Mullā Ṣadrā

MAKERS OF ISLAMIC CIVILIZATION

Series editor: Farhan A. Nizami

This series, conceived by the Oxford Centre for Islamic Studies, is published and distributed by Oxford University Press (India). The books in the series, written by leading scholars in the field, aim to provide an introduction to outstanding figures in the history of Islamic civilization. They will serve as the essential first point of reference for study of the persons, events and ideas that have shaped the Islamic world and the cultural resources on which Muslims continue to draw.

Mullā Ṣadrā

Ibrahim Kalin

Oxford Centre for Islamic Studies

OXFORD
UNIVERSITY PRESS

OXFORD
UNIVERSITY PRESS

Oxford University Press is a department of the University of Oxford. It furthers the University's objective of excellence in research, scholarship, and education by publishing worldwide. Oxford is a registered trademark of Oxford University Press in the UK and in certain other countries

Published in India by
Oxford University Press
YMCA Library Building, 1, Jai Singh Road, New Delhi 110001, India

First edition published in 2014

ISBN-13: 978-0-19-945117-3
ISBN-10: 0-19-945117-6

Cover design: Grace Fussell, Oxford Centre for Islamic Studies
Cover photo: Columns of Vakil Mosque, Shiraz. © Aleksei Kripka

Printed in India by Sapra Brothers, New Delhi 110 092

To Seyyed Hossein Nasr
unfailing mentor, scholar, friend

Contents

1

Introduction

Muḥammad ibn Ibrāhīm ibn Yaḥyā Qawāmī al-Shīrāzī (1570/71–1635 or 1640), known more commonly as Ṣadr al-Dīn al-Shīrāzī and Mullā Ṣadrā, is one of the most important figures of post-Avicennan Islamic philosophy and certainly the most prominent philosopher of Safavid Persia (1501–1722). Ṣadrā is best known for his major contributions to Islamic philosophy and the revival of the study of existence as the foundation of metaphysics and epistemology. Ṣadrā's thought represents a paradigm shift in Islamic philosophy from the Aristotelian metaphysics of fixed substances, which the Muslim Peripatetics had largely adopted, to a vision of reality based on the dynamic and all-encompassing reality of existence (*wujūd*). Ṣadrā's fundamental insight that existence is the source of all things led him to the conclusion that a proper study of metaphysics must begin with existence and end with it. Ṣadrā applied this principle to all issues of philosophy and produced a new and fresh system of thought which he called 'Transcendent Wisdom' (*al-ḥikmat al-muta ͑āliya*).

Already a well-known and respected philosopher in his lifetime, Mullā Ṣadrā influenced generations of philosophers, theologians and scholars from the religious and intellectual circles of Iran to the subcontinent of India. In his homeland Iran, he is embraced as a national hero, a synthesis of the various currents of the Islamic intellectual tradition, and a symbol of the possible union of a rigorous mind and a devout heart. His works are read both as textbooks of traditional philosophy and as a source of inspiration for spiritual refinement. He has been and remains a dominant, towering presence in the Persian intellectual scene, referred to alike in academic discussions of philosophy and in the speeches of Iranian politicians. While some take his ethics to be the basis of a philosophical spirituality, others interpret his natural philosophy as a source of social change, the most dramatic form of which took place in the Iranian Revolution of 1979.

Beyond Iran as well as within it, the attention given to Ṣadrā's work by teachers and students of both Islamic and Western philosophy is seen in the rapidly growing volume of literature devoted to it – scholarly books and monographs, articles, dissertations, national and international conferences, symposia and colloquia. Contributions come from all corners of the world including Arab countries, Turkey, Russia, the Indian subcontinent, Japan, Malaysia, Indonesia, Europe and the US. The lively academic interest in Ṣadrā reveals something of the nature of Ṣadrā's multifaceted thought on the one hand, and the state of intellectual quest in modern academia on the other. At a time when we are looking for ways to combine the widely diverse and increasingly disconnected fields of human knowledge, Mullā Ṣadrā promises a restorative vision of reality that is grounded in sound analytical principles, a non-relativistic ethics, and a liberating spirituality.

Besides 'Transcendent Wisdom', Ṣadrā often uses *ʿirfān*, usually rendered as 'gnosis', to describe this unity of thought and vision, thinking and contemplation, knowing and realizing. His thought is firmly rooted in traditional metaphysics; but it is a rootedness with an open horizon – a horizon that reminds us that the truth, while eminently attainable, can never be reduced to our mental constructions of it.

The study of Mullā Ṣadrā is important, first of all, for a proper understanding of the full spectrum of philosophical thinking in the Islamic tradition. The fact that he produced his scholarly work in the seventeenth century, against the background of a wide body of work in philosophy, theology, mysticism and religious sciences, adds a different kind of depth to his thought. As a first-rate intellect deeply rooted in the tradition, Ṣadrā had a firm grasp of the main issues tackled by the thinkers before him. For him, the philosophical tradition went further back than the Greeks and their Hellenic students: philosophy as wisdom and realization had its true origin in 'the niche of prophecy' (*mishkāt al-nubuwwa*). In combining various strands in the history of philosophical and religious ideas to which he was heir, the multidimensional nature of Ṣadrā's thought attests to the richness and maturity of the philosophical tradition in Islam. That tradition developed gradually over a thousand years and took in many elements from other, pre-Islamic sources. It also developed its own terminology, themes, problems and solutions. Studying Ṣadrā serves as an entry point into this rich tradition. It also suggests that this tradition is not about repetition but a rootedness in the principles of unity, continuity and integrity on the one hand while keeping an open horizon on the other.

Secondly, Ṣadrā is no exception to the rule that every serious philosopher is also a good historian of philosophy. His analysis of a concept or idea is usually presented against the background of previous discussions and arguments. Before providing his own answer, Ṣadrā gives an overview of the issue and in some cases quotes from the sources with which he is working. This is extremely valuable because it gives us a chance to see how history of philosophy comes to life at the hands of a thinker of the calibre of Mullā Ṣadrā. His writings are an invaluable source for the history of Islamic philosophy as well as for the diverse interpretations and adaptations of Greek philosophy among Muslim philosophers and Sufis.

Ṣadrā's reworking of the Greek philosophical tradition, in some ways comparable to that of the Peripatetics before him, also belies the Orientalist assumption that rationality as developed by the Greeks could be accommodated only in Europe in its Hellenic, then Christian, and finally secular, versions. The fact that Islam did not, as Europe did, go through Hellenization and secularization does not prove that reason and rationality, and what they entail for philosophy, law, social order, and aesthetics, did not develop in the Islamic tradition. Ṣadrā is a good example of how Greek philosophical ideas can be studied from multiple perspectives and reproduced in ways that conform to the fundamental premises of the Islamic metaphysics of creation and revelation – the two principal ideas which the Greeks did not have.

Thirdly, Ṣadrā introduced a number of novel ideas and concepts. The idea that Muslim philosophers produced few new ideas, that they were content with the well-established norms of the commentary tradition, is simply wrong, and one can cite numerous examples to disprove it. New ideas were continually proposed and old formulations revised, leading to highly critical and engaging discussions from one generation to another. As for Ṣadrā, we might refer, among much else, to his elaborate terminology of 'existence' (*al-wujūd*), 'gradation of existence' (*tashkīk al-wujūd*), 'substantial motion' (*al-ḥaraka al-jawhariyya*), the notion that 'a reality in its simplicity is all things' (*basīṭ al-ḥaqīqa kull al-ashyā'*), and finally the idea that 'the human soul is corporeal in its origination and spiritual in its subsistence' (*jismāniyyat al-ḥuduth rūḥāniyyat al-baqā'*). Ṣadrā was thus part of a living tradition to which he contributed his own, original philosophical ideas.

That said, we should question the notion of 'originality' as it is used about an intellectual tradition. A tradition is a tradition to the extent that it contains elements of change as well as continuity. A system of thought, a culture or civilization, cannot become a tradition without allowing for critical thinking and novel ideas. A tradition in the ordinary historical sense means something handed down from generation to generation, but this 'handing down', done properly, itself constitutes a form of intellectual activity. A tradition cannot be expected to root out all continuity and permanence in the name of novelty for its own sake. The word 'original' itself points in this direction: it relates to 'origin', the beginning from which other things emanate. Therefore, when we say that Mullā Ṣadrā was an original thinker and introduced new ideas, we refer to these two aspects of the tradition whereby Ṣadrā remained anchored in the Islamic intellectual tradition on the one hand, and developed new ideas and concepts out of that tradition on the other.

Last but not least, Ṣadrā is important for what he says. His ideas are relevant for a number of contemporary issues in metaphysics, ontology, epistemology, philosophical cosmology, psychology, the reason–revelation debate and eschatology. Read carefully, Ṣadrā offers much insight into the philosophical problems with which we are concerned today. Needless to say, one should be chary of shallow comparisons and hasty conclusions. No pre-modern philosopher can be compared and contrasted with the moderns without some distortion, deviation or injustice. Yet the issues persist, and they point to the continuity of human thought.

To give a few examples, Ṣadrā's attempt to restructure philosophy around the central reality of existence resonates with Martin Heidegger's project to bring the forgotten question of being or *Dasein* back to Western thought in his celebrated work *Being and Time*. Both philosophers insist on the centrality of existence and reject ontologies grounded in the knowing subject. What each means by existence is, however, very different from the other, and proceeds from fundamentally different premises. For Ṣadrā, existence is neither a 'personal' issue nor a reality whose truth is revealed by the human state. Since the human subject as we understand the term today never had a prominent place in pre-modern philosophy, Ṣadrā's deliberations on existence and its modalities do not lend themselves to the 'existential psychology' of modern existentialism. Furthermore, Ṣadrā treats existence as part of a transcendent metaphysics and refrains from defining it as the ultimate principle. In Ṣadrā, the immediacy and dominance of existence does not overshadow the absolute reality of God.

Ṣadrā's dynamic world-picture has also been compared with process philosophy. In contrast to the Aristotelian world-order, which was based on fixed substances and thus remained rather opaque, quasi-mechanical and one-dimensional, Ṣadrā constructs his cosmology around the dynamic and self-generating reality of existence. In natural philosophy, this is translated into Ṣadrā's insightful concept of 'substantial motion', which takes the world to be in constant motion and change towards a final purposed outcome (*telos*). Instead of treating the physical world as a unity of solid, fixed substances, substantial motion establishes change as the main principle by which all beings including substances move from one state of existence to another. This highly dynamic cosmology has encouraged some scholars to compare substantial motion to process philosophy as formulated by Whitehead and others. While, at first sight, there are certainly points of convergence between the two systems, what Ṣadrā means by 'motion/change' is significantly different from how process philosophers define 'process'.

Ṣadrā's quest for intellectual and spiritual perfection through discursive and realized knowledge led him to traverse the entire spectrum of human thinking. With the exception of mathematical sciences and such specialist disciplines as medicine and chemistry, Ṣadrā wrote extensively on many subjects – philosophy, logic, natural philosophy, Qurʾānic exegesis, spirituality, psychology and eschatology. These diverse fields take the form of three types (or domains) of knowledge: revealed knowledge, discursive reasoning, and spiritual realization. Ṣadrā's thought is based on a synthesis of *qurʾān*, *burhān*, and *ʿirfān*. *Qurʾān* refers to revealed knowledge and is essential for philosophical, religious and spiritual knowledge and certitude. *Burhān* is best represented by the Peripatetic philosophers and their way of thinking, which is indispensable for a logical and demonstrative explanation of the world. Finally, *ʿirfān* corresponds to realized knowledge, the kind of spiritual epistemology that allows for non-discursive types of knowledge.

In contrast to the Peripatetic philosophers and dialectical theologians, Ṣadrā sees no contradiction between these types of knowledge and insists they are complementary: each corresponds to a particular mode of being since Ṣadrā defines knowledge in terms of existence and its modalities. Just as there is an underlying unity of things in the larger scheme of being, different types of knowledge corresponding to multiple states of being complement each other and yield a unified epistemology grounded not in the cognitive competencies of the knowing subject but in the all-inclusive and extra-mental reality of existence.

Following the mystics, Ṣadrā adds that one must realize what one knows because true knowledge cannot just be a mental image or impression. Knowledge (not to be confused with information) is a metaphysical and ethical undertaking that goes beyond dialectic and demonstration. Like many of the philosophically minded Sufis, Ṣadrā sees a perfect harmony between demonstrative and realized truths because, just as reality is interconnected, so are the types of knowledge that correspond to it. When the rational philosopher rejects mystical knowledge on the basis of 'not enough proof', he simply misuses his reason and creates anomalies for himself. True philosophy, says Ṣadrā, is beyond such simplistic dichotomies because 'true demonstration never contradicts realized knowledge'.

Mullā Ṣadrā's greatest single work, his philosophical monument, is called 'The Four Intellectual Journeys in Transcendent Wisdom' (*al-Asfār al-arbaʿa al-ʿaqliyya fī l-ḥikmat al-mutaʿāliya*). Taken as a whole, it provides one of the most comprehensive and profound descriptions of the journey to intellectual truth and spiritual refinement. The image of a 'journey' is central in Ṣadrā's thought and points to the dynamic nature of philosophical reflection. Philosophy is not a mental exercise, nor is the subject disengaged from it as if contemplating the reality of things from the outside. Serious philosophy transforms the philosopher because the truth is a substantive reality and touches the human being as a whole. Yet, this does not reduce truth to something subjective because the truth, however one conceives it, is larger than the mental constructions of the knowing subject. An intellectual-philosophical journey takes the human person through the multiple stages of perception, consciousness and realization within the larger context of being.

In the following pages, we shall follow Ṣadrā's philosophical journey and take a close look at his intellectual world. In analysing Ṣadrā's thought, I provide a context but largely let him speak for himself. Chapter 1 provides a condensed account of Ṣadrā's life, influence and works. Chapter 2 reviews the dominant social and intellectual trends within which Ṣadrā developed as a thinker and composed his works. Chapter 3 introduces Ṣadrā's ontology and how he formulated his concept of existence as the fundamental problem of metaphysics and philosophy. I discuss the ways in which Ṣadrā confronted the three major crises of the Islamic intellectual tradition in ontology, epistemology and methodology. Chapter 4 provides an overview of Ṣadrā's mature thought and assesses the extent to which it succeeded (or not) in arriving at a coherent synthesis.

In keeping with the format for this series, I have used the fewest possible footnotes – publication details for works cited in the notes are presented in the bibliographical listing at the end of this essay. Citations from Ṣadrā's works are referenced within the main text, with volume and page numbers following an abbreviated title. The abbreviations used are as below:

KEY TO MULLĀ ṢADRĀ'S WORKS

Asfār	*al-Ḥikmat al-mutaʿāliya fī l-asfār al-ʿaqliyyat al-arbaʿa* (Beirut: Dār Iḥyāʾ al-Turāth al-ʿArabī, 9 vols., 1981).
Ḥashr	*Risālat al-ḥashr* (ed. and Persian transl. by Muḥammad Khvājavī; Tehran: Intishārat-i Mavlavī, 1998).
Ḥuduth	*Ḥuduth al-ʿālam* (ed. S. H. Musaviyan; Tehran: Bunyād-i Ḥikmat-i Islāmi-yi Ṣadrā [SIPRIn], 1378 SH).
Iksīr	*Iksīr al-ʿārifīn*. Ed. and transl. William Chittick, *The Elixir of the Gnostics* (Provo, UT: Brigham Young University Press, 2003).
Īqāẓ	*Īqāẓ al-nāʾimīn* (ed. Mohammed Khansari; Tehran: SIPRIn, 1384/2005).
Kāshāniyya	*Ajwibat al-masāʾil al-kāshāniyya* in *Majmūʿa*.
Kasr	*Kasr aṣnām al-jāhiliyya* (ed. N. Jihāngīri; Tehran: SIPRIn, 1381 SH).
Mafātiḥ	*Mafātiḥ al-ghayb* (with the glosses of Mulay ʿAlī al-Nūrī; Beirut: Muʾassasat al-Taʾrīkh al-ʿArabī, 2 vols., 1999).
Majmūʿa	*Majmūʿa-yi rasāʾil-i falsafī-yi ṣadr al-mutaʾallihīn* (ed. Ḥāmid Najī Iṣfahānī; Tehran: Intishārat-i Ḥikmat, 1375 SH).
Mashāʿir	*Kitāb al-Mashāʿir*. Ed. and transl. Henry Corbin, *Le Livre des pénétrations métaphysiques* (Tehran: Institut Français d'Iranologie de Téhéran, 1982).
Maẓāhir	*al-Maẓāhir al-ilāhiyya fī asrār al-ʿulūm al-kamāliyya* (ed. S. M. Khamanei; Tehran: SIPRIn, 1378 SH).

Qudsiyya	*al-Masāʾil al-qudsiyya* in *Seh Risāla-i falsafī* (ed. S. J. Ashtiyānī; Qom: Markaz-i Intishārāt-i Daftar-i Tablīghat-i Islāmī, 1379 SH).
Rasāʾil	*Rasāʾil-i falsafī* (ed. Jalāl al-Dīn Ashtiyānī; Qom: 1362 SH).
Sharḥ	*Sharḥ-i ilāhiyyat-i shifāʾ* (ed. Najafqūlī Ḥabībī; Tehran: SIPRIn, 2 vols., 1382 SH).
Shawāhid	*al-Shawāhid al-rubūbiyya* (ed. Sayyid Jalāl al-Dīn Ashtiyānī; Mashhad: al-Markaz al-Jāmiᶜ li-l-Nashr, 2nd edn., 1981).
Tafsīr	*Tafsīr al-Qurʾān al-karīm* (ed. Muḥammad Khvājavī; Qom: Bidar Press, 7 vols., 1987–90).
Taṣawwur	*Risālat al-taṣawwur wa-l-taṣdīq in Risālatān fī l-taṣawwur wa-l-taṣdīq* (ed. Mahdī Shariᶜatī; Beirut: Dār al-Kutub al-ᶜIlmiyya, 2004).
Uṣūl	*Sharḥ Uṣūl al-kāfī (K. al-ᶜAql wa-l-jahl)* (ed. Muḥammad Khvājavī; Tehran: n.p., 5 vols., 1366 SH).

1

Ṣadrā's life, influence and works

Ṣadrā was born in Shiraz in 979–80/1571–72 into a relatively prosperous family, his father being a court employee of the Safavid state. His life was largely settled and stable, with access to a good education and an environment that was scholarly as well as political. Though his father was involved in the political life of the Safavid court, Ṣadrā himself showed not the least interest in politics – he never held any government position or took any part in affairs of state. Even his interest in the science of politics is fairly limited. The trajectory of his worldly life was not marked by the kind of excitement, travels and travails of an Ibn Sīnā (Avicenna), Ibn Khaldūn or Ibn Baṭṭūta. Perhaps he believed, like Socrates, that a true philosopher or lover of wisdom has no real business in political life. But as we shall see, Ṣadrā suffered from a different kind of politics at the hands of some arrogant scholars and the pretentious ascetics whom he called 'pseudo-Sufis' (*al-mutaṣawwifa*).

His early education consisted mainly of the so-called traditional or 'transmitted' sciences (*al-ʿulūm al-naqliyya*), which included Arabic grammar, Qurʾānic exegesis (*tafsīr*), jurisprudence (*fiqh*), and the traditions of the Prophet (*ʿilm al-ḥadīth*). These sciences were an integral part of Ṣadrā's intellectual upbringing. Prompted by his intellectual and spiritual thirst, he left his hometown for Qazvin, the capital of the Safavid Empire at the time. When Shāh ʿAbbās I moved the capital to Isfahan in 1597 (under pressure from the Ottomans), Ṣadrā, still in his teens, followed the caravan. In these major centres of learning, philosophy, art and politics, he studied the so-called 'rational' sciences' (*al-ʿulūm al-ʿaqliyya*), i.e., logic, theology, philosophy, metaphysics and natural philosophy, and began to lay the foundations of the philosophical edifice that he would spend his life building. He studied with two prominent masters: Sayyid Bāqir Muḥammad Astarābādī, known as Mīr Dāmād (d. 1631), and Bahāʾ al-Dīn Muḥammad al-ʿĀmilī known as Shaykh Bahāʾī (d. 1622). Both scholars left an enduring impact on Ṣadrā's intellectual upbringing and spiritual quest and shaped his thinking even when he parted ways with them on a number of key philosophical issues.

After completing his philosophical training in Isfahan, Ṣadrā retreated to Kahak, a small village near Qom. We do not have much detail about this self-imposed exile. Some of Ṣadrā's autobiographical remarks suggest that the hostility of the literalist-exotericist scholars in Isfahan played a part in his decision. We do not know if Ṣadrā's opponents were motivated by simple jealousy or by political or other considerations. But it is clear that Ṣadrā was tired of their attacks and decided to leave the great city of Isfahan even though he was probably just then making a name for himself among its scholarly circles. It was during this time that he fully immersed himself in the Greek-Peripatetic and Illuminationist schools of thought on the one hand

and, on the other, the metaphysical doctrines of the Sufis, especially the school of Ibn ʿArabī. Ṣadrā recalls this time not in terms of personal or political rivalry but in terms of an intellectual confrontation between different paths of thinking: his own philosophical vocation, then just taking shape, and the simplistic and anti-intellectualist approach of the literalists and the pseudo-ascetics. Particularly offensive to the literalists was Ṣadrā's embrace of transmitted sciences and metaphysical and mystical ideas. Even though Ṣadrā did not directly and actively engage in the most important controversy of Safavid Shiʿism in the eleventh/seventeenth century, between the Akhbārīs and the Uṣūlīs, his intellectual outlook put him at odds with the increasingly literalist and legalist attitude of the former. To understand the impact that confrontation had on Ṣadrā's thought, we need to take a quick look at the Akhbārī–Uṣūlī debate.

THE AKHBĀRĪ–UṢŪLĪ CONTROVERSY

When Ṣadrā began his philosophical career, a major rift had emerged between two schools of thought in Safavid Persia. The Shiʿi scholars known as Uṣūlīs upheld the principle of reason and personal opinion on religious-legal issues and welcomed philosophical debates. They were fiercely opposed by a group of scholars who came to be known as Akhbārīs. Grounded in a pietistic anti-intellectualism, the Akhbārī traditionalism-cum-literalism was opposed to philosophical and mystical interpretations of the Qurʾān and of the sayings of the Prophet of Islam, and those of Shiʿi Imams. Its followers considered it sufficient to rely on the literal authority of the sayings or 'reports' (*akhbār*, plural of *khabar*, hence the name *Akhbārī*) of the Imams, bolstering, in turn, the socio-religious status of rulers and scholars who claimed family descent from those Imams. But they also opposed philosophy as a redundant, even harmful, enterprise as it suggested that all texts, including religious ones, require an interpretative reader, implying that the texts by themselves are incomplete. In order to show that the 'reports' were sufficient as a foundation for understanding faith and living religion, the famous Akhbārī scholar Muḥammad Bāqir Majlisī wrote a monumental work called *Bihār al-anwār* (Ocean of Lights) which, in its modern edition of 176 volumes, contains all of the available reports narrated from the Shiʿi Imams and other scholars.

The Akhbārī–Uṣūlī dispute became bitter and reached a climax in the seventeenth century especially with the revival of Akhbārīsm by Mullā Muḥammad Amīn ibn Muḥammad Sharīf of Astarabad (d. 1623–4). The Akhbārīs gained the favour of the Safavid court until the reign of Shāh Ṣafī (1629–42) and Shāh ʿAbbās II (1642–66). Their opponents gave them such disparaging names as the 'people of the exterior' (*ahl-i ẓāhir*) and the 'scholars of the skin or surface' (*ʿulamā-yi qishr*). Like the Sunni school of Ahl al-Ḥadīth, known for their opposition to any report, opinion or judgment other than what is reported in the hadith collections, the Akhbārīs defended a strict and narrow interpretation of the sayings of the Shiʿi Imams and rejected other types of knowledge as *bidʿa*, pernicious innovation, not approved by the canonical sources. As a result, they attacked the intellectual sciences and those who embraced them in the name of religious orthodoxy and piety.

Ṣadrā does not mention any Akhbārīs by name but it is clear that he had his share of their hostility because of his philosophical and metaphysical views. In the *Asfār*, he compares them to the Hanbali scholars of hadith who are known for their strict literalism and anti-intellectualism. They have shunned philosophy and banned metaphysics, Ṣadrā complains, all in the name of protecting God's religion but in reality '[God's] prophets and saints have explained and the sage-philosophers and gnostics have referred to the path of wisdom and certitude in the sacred Divine sciences and noble secrets', which these dogmatic literalists have denounced as an 'innovation' (*bidʿa*) (*Asfār*, i. 6).

In his *Kasr aṣnām al-jāhiliyya* (Destroying the Idols of Ignorance), he criticizes the pseudo-Sufis and pretentious ascetics of his time and admonishes them for giving up sapiential knowledge in the name of pure asceticism. Without the knowledge of the truth, Ṣadrā held, no ascetic ritual has meaning, and only 'mediocre pretentious mystics' (*ʿāmmat al-mutaṣawwifa*) and 'ordinary preachers' (*ʿawāmm al-wuʿāẓ*) can make such baseless claims (*Kasr*, 44). While attacking pretentious Sufis, Ṣadrā also criticizes the Akhbārīs for their claim that they can reach a level of religious purity without philosophical reflection. Contrary to what the Akhbārīs allege, the reports and texts, including the Qurʾān and the hadith, on which the literalists rely, invite and encourage deep reflection and meditation on God's creation. The intimate 'knowledge of God' (*maʿrifat Allāh*), which is the highest form of truth, can be attained only through reflection and purification.

In contrast to the Akhbārīs, the Uṣūlīs held that a proper understanding of the religious tradition entailed a firm grasp of the 'principles' (*uṣūl*, sing. *aṣl*; hence the name 'Uṣūlī') of the religion as established by the Qurʾān, the Prophet and His followers. Understanding these principles requires an interpretative exercise in religious texts and involves the use of hermeneutical tools. The Uṣūlīs saw no contradiction between text and interpretation even though the precise nature of their relationship was to be worked out through textual verification and conceptual analysis. By accepting a relationship of complementarity between the two, they created a space for interpretation, critical thinking and textual analysis. This meant the acceptance of the multi-layered meanings and multiple readings of a text including religious ones. With the work of the prominent Uṣūlī scholar Āqā Muḥammad Bāqir Bihbahānī (1704–1793), who went so far as to call the Akhbārīs 'unbelievers', the Uṣūlīs won the argument in Safavid Persia and the study of philosophical sciences continued unabated. But just like the Ahl al-Ḥadīth in the Sunni world, Akhbārī attitudes continued as an under-current among some Shiʿi scholars. Akhbārī literalism, while having some influence in the sixteenth and seventeenth centuries, never became so powerful a movement as to deter such great minds as Mīr Dāmād, Shaykh Bahāʾī, Mīr Findiriskī, Fayḍ Kāshānī, and numerous others, from profound philosophical study and spiritual reflection.

During his years in Kahak, Ṣadrā continued his studies in solitude and began to compose some of his major works. We know very little about his time in Kahak but it is clear that it was here that Ṣadrā developed the key arguments of his philosophy and laid the ground for his magnum opus, *Asfār*. After this solitary period, which fits perfectly with the initial stations of the intellectual-spiritual journey outlined in the *Asfār*, Ṣadrā returned to Shiraz to teach at the Khān madrasa built for him by Allāhvirdī Khān. The third phase of Ṣadrā's life began here in the Khān madrasa, a building still extant in Shiraz. Ṣadrā composed and completed his major works and trained his choice students in this simple yet beautiful school. As a devout Muslim philosopher, he went on pilgrimage on foot six times, and died in Basra in 1045/1635-6 or 1050/1640 on his seventh ḥajj to Makka. He was buried in Najaf, Iraq, within the same compound that houses the tomb of Imam ʿAlī ibn Abī Ṭālib.

STUDENTS AND INFLUENCE

Mullā Ṣadrā left a deep impact on Persian intellectual and religious circles and had considerable influence in the subcontinent of India. This is registered in the numerous students and followers he has had over the last four centuries and in the references to his ideas in various works of philosophy, theology and mysticism. His influence is also reflected in the honorific titles given to him such as *ṣadr al-dīn*. The word *ṣadr* (lit. chest, bosom), signifies the 'heart and source' and 'being foremost'. The title *ṣadr al-dīn* coveys the authority of one who has attained the heart of truth by his eminence in the *dīn*, religion. *Ṣadr al-mutaʾallihīn*, another major title given to him, means 'foremost among those who have become Divine-like'. The word *mutaʾallih*, 'becoming Divine-like', goes back to Shihāb al-Dīn Suhrawardī, the founder of the School of Illumination, and has a specific referent in Suhrawardī's triple classification of the types of human thought and knowledge. The *mutaʾallih*, whom Suhrawardī identifies as 'God's real vicegerent on earth' (*khalīfat Allāh*), is the philosopher-sage or godly philosopher who has combined rational inquiry with spiritual realization. Finally, some sources refer to Ṣadrā with the Persian title *akhund*, meaning a deeply learned person.

Ṣadrā's students and followers wrote commentaries on his works, expanded his ideas, refined his original contributions to philosophy, and became prominent scholars and intellectuals in their own right. Mullā Muḥsin Fayḍ Kāshānī (d. 1680) and

ʿAbd al-Razzāq ibn al-Ḥusayn Lāhijī (d. 1662) were Ṣadrā's two most famous students. Fayḍ Kāshānī authored *Uṣūl al-maʿārif* and *al-Kalimat al-maknūna*, both of which further expounded Ṣadrā's teachings. Lāhijī wrote important works of Twelve-Imam Shiʿi *kalām*, among which *Gawhar-i murād* and *Shawāriq al-ilhām* are of particular importance. Both Kāshānī and Lāhijī married daughters of Ṣadrā and carried their master–disciple relationship to a personal level, and trained important figures of the school of Mullā Ṣadrā such as Qāḍī Saʿīd Qummī.

As Ṣadrā's ideas spread in the Persian and Indian worlds in the post-Safavid era, Ṣadrā came to have many followers from diverse intellectual circles. In the philosophical circles of Iran, one can mention Āqā Muḥammad Bīdābādī (d. 1783), Qāḍī Saʿīd Qummī (18th c.), Mullā ʿAlī ibn Jamshīd Nūrī (d. 1830), Mullā Muḥammad Ismāʿīl Iṣfahānī (d. 1860), Mullā ʿAbdullāh Zunūzī (19th c.), Mullā Muḥammad Jaʿfar Langarūdī Lāhijī (19th c.), Mullā Ismāʿīl Khājūʾī (19th c.), Mullā Hādī Sabziwārī (d. 1873), Mullā ʿAbdullāh Zunūzī and his son Āqā ʿAlī Mudarris Zunūzī (d. 1889), Āqā Muḥammad Riḍā Qumshāʾī (d. 1888-9), and Mīrzā Mahdī Ashtiyānī (19th c.). Among traditional scholars of the twentieth century, we should mention Muḥammad Ḥusayn Ṭabāṭabāʾī (d. 1981), the author of the monumental Qurʾānic commentary *Tafsīr al-Mīzān*, Sayyid Abū l-Ḥasan Qazwīnī (d. 1975), a well-known master of traditional philosophy and the school of Mullā Ṣadrā, and Muḥammad Kāzim ʿAṣṣār (d. 1975), the author of an important work on traditional Islamic philosophy titled *Thalāth Rasāʾil fī l-ḥikma al-islāmiyya.*

Ṣadrā influenced scholars and intellectuals outside the traditional madrasa or *ḥawza* circles. Murtada Mutahhari, Mahdi Hairi Yazdi, Abd al-Karim Soroush, Ghulam

Reza A'wani, Ibrahim Dinani, Mohammad Khwajawi, S. Mohammad Khamanei and Abdullah Jawadi Amuli are among the prominent Iranian scholars who have studied and further articulated Ṣadrā's ideas. The late Seyyed Jalāl al-Dīn Ashtiyānī published Ṣadrā's works in uncritical yet useful editions and authored several works of his own to expound Ṣadrā's ideas. Seyyed Hossein Nasr, who studied the philosophy of Mullā Ṣadrā with such traditional masters as Abū l-Ḥasan Qazwīnī and Kāzim ʿAṣṣār, played a leading role in the introduction of Ṣadrā's ideas to Western academic circles and produced a lucid analysis of the school of Mullā Ṣadrā in a number of studies published since the 1960s. The Ṣadrā Islamic Philosophy Research Institute (SIPRIn) under the presidency of Mohammad Khamanei has undertaken the important task of publishing Ṣadrā's works in critical editions, organizing meetings and conferences and supporting research on Ṣadrā.

ṢADRĀ AND POSTERITY

'Influence' comes in different ways and there is no simple way of measuring it. Ṣadrā's ideas have attracted scores of students, seekers of knowledge, academic philosophers and even social and political actors over the last four centuries. While Ṣadrā had no 'revolutionary' agenda in the modern political sense of the term, his dynamic metaphysics and cosmology have been invoked in the context of the Iranian revolution of 1979. Some Iranian intellectuals have referred to Ṣadrā's notion of 'substantial motion' to explain the dynamics of social change and argued that true change, i.e., revolution, must come from within the society and its core values – a clear reference to Ṣadrā's theory that change takes place not only in the accidents of things but also in their substance. Applied to sociology and political science, substantial motion becomes a heuristic model to explain how social change does and, in a revolutionary context must, take place.

Ṣadrā's life in the Iranian political scene is not limited to intellectuals. Like many religious and intellectual figures over the last four centuries in Iran, Ayatollah Khomeini, the leader of the Islamic revolution of Iran, studied Mullā Ṣadrā and incorporated Ṣadrā's philosophical ideas into his work. His books and sermons contain references to Mullā Ṣadrā and in particular to the 'Four Journeys', around which Ṣadrā builds his 'Transcendent Wisdom'. In one of the most striking stories of recent politics, Ṣadrā's name comes up in a letter sent by Ayatollah Khomeini to Mikhail Gorbachev in 1989. In it, Ayatollah Khomeini invites Gorbachev, who was leading the Perestroika movement in his country, to look beyond communism and have Soviet scholars study such traditional Muslim philosophers as al-Fārābī, Ibn Sīnā, Suhrawardī and Ibn ʿArabī. Not surprisingly, the list included Mullā Ṣadrā. Ayatollah Khomeini's *Misbāḥ al-hidāya ilā l-khilāfa wa-l-wilāya* (The Lamp of Guidance for Vicegerency and Sainthood), an important work on spirituality and political theology, which he wrote long before the Iranian revolution, contains numerous references to Ṣadrā's *Asfār* as well as such prominent members of the school of Ibn ʿArabī as Ṣadr al-Dīn al-Qūnawī and Dāʾūd al-Qayṣarī.

Outside Persia, Ṣadrā had a considerable following in the subcontinent of India. Although the full scale of his influence in India has yet to be studied, two important figures deserve attention. Shāh Walīullāh of Delhi (1702–1762), the greatest Muslim scholar of India in the eighteenth century, composed works in both religious and philosophical sciences and played a central role in the spiritual, social and political life of the Muslims of India. Like those of Ṣadrā, Shāh Walīullāh's works and particularly his *Ḥujjat Allāh al-bāligha* represent an impressive synthesis of religious knowledge, jurisprudence, philosophy, logic, theology and Sufism. In his attempt to formulate an integrated epistemology, Shāh Walīullāh adopts Ṣadrā's outlook on the unity of religious and intellectual sciences, revelation and reason, and intuition and logical thinking.

In the twentieth century, Ashraf ᶜAlī Thānwī (1863–1943), known among Indian Muslims as *Ḥakīm al-umma* ('the sage of the Muslim community') studied Mullā Ṣadrā and made extensive use of his works in his critical treatment of modernism. Like his predecessors, ᶜAlī Thānwī was a philosopher, theologian, jurist and Sufi all at once. In his refutation of modern materialism, he refers his readers to his own philosophical work *Dirāyat al-ᶜiṣma* and to Mullā Ṣadrā's well-known *Sharḥ Hidāyat al-ḥikma*, a commentary on the famous book of formal logic by Athīr al-Dīn Abharī. This commentary is probably the most widely read work of Ṣadrā in the subcontinent of India though his other works have also been studied, as evidenced by the large number of the manuscripts of Ṣadrā's works in various libraries in India.

To the list of prominent figures who have studied the works of Ṣadrā in India, one can also add Muhammad Iqbal, the great Muslim poet and philosopher of Muslim India and the spiritual father of modern Pakistan. Iqbal's influence on the intellectual, social, and political life of Indian Muslims has been unmistakable, and he remains a source of inspiration for Muslims around the world. Although one cannot count Iqbal among the followers of Mullā Ṣadrā in the philosophical sense of the term, his works contain elements from Ṣadrā's teachings. *The Development of Metaphysics in Persia*, which Iqbal prepared as a doctoral dissertation, shows his familiarity with Ṣadrā's ideas. Like Ṣadrā, Iqbal espouses a dynamic view of the universe and seeks to combine rational and mystical methods of attaining the truth. Ṣadrā's influence in India is also underlined by the rather little known fact that Mawlānā Mawdūdī, the founder of the Jamaᶜat-i Islami of Pakistan and one of the most influential political thinkers of twentieth-century Islam, translated parts of the *Asfār* into Urdu.

Jamāl al-Dīn al-Afghānī (d. 1897), the most famous political activist of the nineteenth-century Muslim world and the main source of inspiration for the pan-Islamist movement, studied Mullā Ṣadrā as part of his intellectual training. Even though Afghānī the activist spent most of his life travelling in the Muslim world and mobilizing Muslims to unite, Afghānī the thinker was engaged in an intellectual battle against Western materialism and Eurocentrism. In his *Hakīkat-i madhhab-i naycharī wa-bayān-i ḥāl-i naychariyān*, first published in Haydarabad-Deccan in 1881 and translated into Arabic by Muḥammad ᶜAbdūh as *al-Radd ᶜalā l-dahriyyīn* (The Refutation of the Materialists), Afghānī identifies materialism as the greatest threat to human civilization and attempts to refute its philosophical foundations. His arguments are based largely on the proofs of traditional Islamic philosophy and also display his familiarity with the work of Mullā Ṣadrā.

THE ACADEMIC STUDY OF MULLĀ ṢADRĀ

Academic interest in Ṣadrā studies in the West has a surprisingly long history. In Europe, Comte de Gobineau's *Les Religions et les philosophies dans l'Asie central*, published in 1866, is the earliest work to refer to Mullā Ṣadrā. The German scholar Max Horten is the first European scholar to have devoted a separate work on Ṣadrā. Horten's *Die Gottesbeweise bei Shīrāzī* (Bonn, 1912) and *Das philosophische System von Shīrāzī* (Strasburg, 1913) presents a fairly complete analysis of his system with translations from Ṣadrā's works.

The French philosopher and Islamicist Henry Corbin, who had started his career in Western philosophy by translating Heidegger's *Sein und Zeit* into French, played a leading role in making Ṣadrā's ideas available to academic and non-academic circles in Europe. Corbin translated *Kitāb al-Mashā*ʿ*ir* into French under the title *Le Livre des pénétrations métaphysiques* (Tehran-Paris, 1956) with an extensive analysis of Ṣadrā's thought and a parallel commentary on the *Mashā*ʿ*ir*. In addition to devoting a large section to Ṣadrā in his *En islam iranien: aspects spirituels et philosophiques* (4 vols., 1971–2: iv. 54–122), Corbin also made a partial translation of Ṣadrā's commentary on Suhrawardī's *Ḥikmat al-ishrāq* along with Quṭb al-Dīn Shīrāzī 's commentary in his *Le Livre de la sagesse orientale* (Lagrasse: Editions Verdier, 1986).

Seyyed Hossein Nasr has written a number of seminal essays on Ṣadrā in addition to his book *Ṣadr al-Dīn al-Shīrāzī and His Transcendent Theosophy* (first published 1978; second expanded edition 1997). Fazlur Rahman's *The Philosophy of Mullā Ṣadrā* (Albany: State University of New York Press, 1975) deals with Ṣadrā's philosophy as a whole from a primarily analytic-Peripatetic point of view. At the present time, the scholars producing serious writing on Ṣadrā and/or translating Ṣadrā's works into European languages include Alparslan Açıkgenç, Reza Akbarian, Cecile Bonmariage, David Burrell, Caner Dagli, Janis Esots, Christian Jambet, Muḥammad Kamal, Oliver Leaman, Parviz Morewedge, James Winston Morris, Zailan Moris, Shahram Pazouki,

Latimah-Parvin Peervani, Sajjad Rizvi, Mohammed Rustom and Bagher Talgharizadeh.

WORKS

Mullā Ṣadrā was a prolific writer. His works range from the nine-volume *Asfār* and seven-volume unfinished Qurʾānic commentary to mid-size works such as *Ḥuduth al-ʿālam* and short treatises. With the exception of his *Sih aṣl* (The Three Principles) and a *dīwān* of poetry in Persian, Ṣadrā wrote all of his works in Arabic. As a general trait of his philosophy, Ṣadrā weaves together the strictly logical discourse of the Peripatetic philosophers with the ecstatic language of the mystics. It is not uncommon to see Ṣadrā bursting into aphorisms, exhortations, and ecstatic exclamations while discussing a particular philosophical or cosmological problem in a rigorously analytical manner. In cases where prose seems inadequate to convey his intended meaning, Ṣadrā does not hesitate to quote poetry in Arabic and Persian.

Ṣadrā's works span the entire spectrum of traditional philosophy. The main issues in metaphysics, cosmology, ontology, theology, epistemology, axiology, eschatology, psychology and natural philosophy are treated in their traditional formats. The central theme of these works is the 'primacy of existence' (*aṣālat al-wujūd*), and it penetrates his philosophical as well as religious writings. Ṣadrā's working principle is that no meaningful metaphysics and epistemology is possible without first developing a proper ontology. Whether commenting on a verse from the Qurʾān or discussing types of knowledge, Ṣadrā always comes back to the principle of existence and grounds everything in its all-inclusive reality. Like all traditional philosophers, he quotes freely from previous thinkers, provides commentaries, contrasts his views with others, and develops new themes through lengthy discussions. Reading through the Ṣadrean corpus is like taking a journey in the universal history of philosophy: one is constantly listening to ancient Greeks, referring to pre-Islamic sages of the East, arguing with Muslim Peripatetics, refuting or agreeing with Ashʿari or Muʿtazili theologians, hearing the mystics, and always being reminded that the ultimate goal of philosophy is not mental gymnastics but the attainment of intellectual and spiritual perfection.

Works in the transmitted sciences

Ṣadrā's writings, considering their types and the disciplines in which they have been composed, can be grouped under the two main categories of 'transmitted sciences' and 'intellectual sciences'. The first category of works consists of Ṣadrā's unfinished commentaries on the Qurʾān, the Shiʿi book of hadith called *Uṣūl al-kāfi,* and his books on the hermeneutics of the Qurʾān. The Qurʾānic commentary comprises Ṣadrā's glosses of uneven length on the following chapters and verses of the Qurʾān: *al-Fātiḥa*, the opening chapter of the Qurʾān, *al-Baqara* (2) up to verse 65, *Āyat al-kursī* (2: 255), *Āyat al-nūr* (24: 35), *al-Sajda* (32), *Yā Sīn* (36), *al-Wāqiʿa* (56), *al-Ḥadīd* (57), *al-Jumūʿa* (62), *al-Ṭāriq* (86), *al-Aʿlā* (87), *al-Zilzāl* (99) and *al-Tawḥīd* or *al-Ikhlāṣ* (112).

These commentaries have been edited by M. Khvajavi in seven volumes as *Tafsīr al-Qurʾān al-Karīm* of Mullā Ṣadrā. They showcase Ṣadrā's immense knowledge of the traditional sciences of Qurʾānic exegesis, the hadith, Arabic grammar, Islamic jurisprudence, history of Islam, and other traditional disciplines. Ṣadrā's *Tafsīr* is one of the most outstanding examples of philosophical commentary and weaves together transmitted and intellectual sciences. It is the work of a devout philosophical mind, combining profound understanding of revealed knowledge with a mastery of philosophical thinking.

Besides the *Tafsīr*, Ṣadrā has written two major works on the hermeneutics of the Qurʾān. *Mafātiḥ al-ghayb* (Keys of the Invisible World) contains the most extensive discussion of Ṣadrā's notion of the interpretation of the Qurʾān and combines religious and metaphysical investigation in a typically Ṣadrean fashion. The topics discussed include the reason for the creation of the universe, the Divine intention in sending the Qurʾān, knowledge and its degrees, God's Names and Attributes, a complete exposition of the cosmos from the angels to the minerals, and man's journey from birth to resurrection. *Mutashābihāt al-Qurʾān* (The Allegorical Verses of the Qurʾān) is an in-depth exposition of the Qurʾānic verses that are called allegorical or metaphorical (*mutashābih*) by the Qurʾān (*Āl ʿImrān*, 3: 7) such as 'God sitting on the Throne' and 'God's hand'. It is also a very refined statement of Ṣadrā's theology and shows the extent to which Ṣadrā engages and criticizes previous commentators and theologians. Of particular importance is the discussion of *tanzīh* ('transcendence'), *tashbīh* ('immanence') and *taʿṭīl* ('suspension' of any attributes in regard to God). Ṣadrā rejects 'suspension' as illogical and inconsistent with the Qurʾān, defending, instead, a balanced view of seeing God as both transcendent and immanent. Finally, Ṣadrā gives his own interpretation of some of the allegorical verses and provides a very refined example of exegetical theology.

Another major work in the category of transmitted sciences is *Sharḥ Uṣūl al-kāfī: K. al-ʿAql wa-l-jahl* (Commentary on the *Uṣūl al-kāfī*: the Book of Intellect and Ignorance), which is a philosophical commentary on the famous Shiʿi book of hadith compiled by Abū Jaʿfar Muḥammad ibn

Yaʿqūb Kulaynī (d. 329/940). The main issues include the meaning and degrees of the intellect (*al-ʿaql*) and ignorance (*al-jahl*), God's Essence, Names and Attributes, the cosmos and its creation, relation between the intellect and the heart (*al-qalb*), and the role of the intellect in achieving happiness. This is followed by the longest commentary of the book on hadith no. 14 that 'God has created the intellect'. Here Ṣadrā goes into a detailed discussion of the subject by quoting a number of sayings of the Shiʿi Imams from other sources. This commentary illustrates once again Ṣadrā's integrated approach to religious and intellectual sciences.

Philosophical works

Ṣadrā composed a large number of works in the field of philosophical sciences. Here I shall mention only the most important ones. Ṣadrā's magnum opus is *al-Ḥikmat al-mutaʿāliya fī l-asfār al-ʿaqliyya al-arbaʿa* (The Transcendent Wisdom in the Four Intellectual Journeys), known as *Asfār*. Written in four parts, i.e., 'four journeys', the *Asfār* is a tour de force of post-Avicennan Islamic philosophy. With the exception of logic which Ṣadrā addresses in other works, it covers the entire spectrum of traditional philosophy from ontology and epistemology to psychology and eschatology. The image of 'journeying' (*safar*) is taken without doubt from the Qurʾān and the later Sufi tradition. The first of the 'four journeys' is 'from the world of creation to the Truth' (*min al-khalq ilā l-ḥaqq*) where the fundamental questions of metaphysics and ontology are introduced. It is here that our philosopher presents the ontological foundations of his thought including such topics as the meaning and goal of philosophy, the primacy of existence, essence (*māhiyya*), gradation of existence (*tashkīk al-wujūd*), mental existence (*al-wujūd al-dhihnī*), Platonic Forms, causality, substantial movement, time, the temporal origination of the world, and the unification of the intellect with the intelligible.

The second journey is 'from the Truth to the Truth by the Truth' (*min al-ḥaqq ilā l-ḥaqq bi-l-ḥaqq*) where we find the full account of Ṣadrā's natural philosophy and his detailed critique of the ten Aristotelian categories. Issues discussed include the categories, substance and accidents, how physical entities come to exist, *hylé* and its philosophical significance, matter and form (hylomorphism), natural forms, and the hierarchy of the physical universe.

The third journey is 'from the Truth to the world of creation with the Truth' (*min al-ḥaqq ilā l-khalq bi-l-ḥaqq*) where Ṣadrā goes into his reconstruction of theology. It is in this part of the *Asfār* that Ṣadrā lays out his theology and provides a critique of the theologians. Among the issues he addresses are the unity and existence of God and the previous *kalām* proofs given of it, the ontological simplicity of the Necessary Being, the Names and Qualities of God, God's knowledge of the world, His power, Divine providence, speech (*kalām*) as a Divine quality, good and evil (theodicy), procession of the world of multiplicity from the One, and the unity of philosophy (*ḥikma*) and Divine Law (*sharīʿa*).

The fourth and final journey is 'from the world of creation to the world of creation with the Truth' (*min al-khalq ilā l-khalq bi-l-ḥaqq*) where the great chain of being is completed with psychology, resurrection, and eschatology. This has two closely related meanings in Ṣadrā's thought. First, the intellectual journey of the 'traveller' (*sālik*) continues in the present and posthumous state of human beings. Second, the material and spiritual journey of the order of existence, which begins with the creation of the world and the reality of being, is brought to full completion in its ultimate return to God. This part of the *Asfār* provides a *tour de force* investigation of traditional psychology with material culled from the Peripatetic psychology of Ibn Sīnā and the spiritual anthropology of Ibn ʿArabī. The issues discussed include the soul and its states, various powers of the soul in its interaction with physical and intelligible worlds, sense perception, 'imagination' (*takhayyul*) and the 'imaginal world' (*ʿālam al-khayāl*). Ṣadrā also discusses his celebrated doctrine that 'the soul is bodily in its origination and spiritual in its subsistence' (*jismāniyyat al-ḥuduth ruḥāniyyat al-bāqāʾ*), the impossibility of 'transmigration' (*tanāsukh*), spiritual and bodily resurrection, and heaven and hell.

The four parts or 'journeys' of the *Asfār* roughly correspond to the four main areas of ontology, cosmology, theology and psychology. According to his own statement, Ṣadrā has written the *Asfār* with the philosophers in mind, i.e., the Peripatetic philosophers. *Asfār*'s discursive-analytical nature is unmistakable, and Ṣadrā shows his mastery of philosophical argumentation. But his main point is that Peripatetic philosophy, taken to its logical conclusion, ends up in Platonism and leads to philosophy as spiritual exercise. This point is further articulated in Ṣadrā's other philosophical and mystical works. Among these, we can mention *al-Shawāhid al-rubūbiyya fī l-manāhij al-sulūkiyya* (The Divine Witnesses in the Paths of Spiritual Journeying), a work on ontology and metaphysics with a discussion of the 'science of the return of all things to God' (*ʿilm al-maʿād*), bodily resurrection, the hereafter, prophetology (*al-nubuwwa*) and sainthood (*al-wilāya*). *Al-Maẓāhir al-ilāhiyya fī asrār al-ʿulūm al-kamāliyya* (Divine Manifestations concerning the Secrets of the Sciences of Perfection) is a theological work synthesizing philosophical arguments with quotations from the Qurʾān. *Kitāb al-Mashāʿir* (The Book of Metaphysical Penetrations) is a late work in which Ṣadrā gives a summa of his ontology with short and dense discussions of some theological issues. *Mashāʿir* has been widely taught in philosophical circles and commented upon by later scholars.

Works in cosmology, eschatology and Sufism

Ṣadrā has probably written more on cosmology than any other figure among the Muslim philosophers. He sees cosmology as an extension of ontology and applies the principle of the primacy of existence to all aspects of cosmology, cosmogony and eschatology. *Al-Mabdaʾ wa-l-maʿād* (The Beginning and the Return) treats cosmogony and eschatology as part of the great chain of being and discusses the main divisions of traditional philosophy including metaphysics, natural philosophy, psychology, the genesis of the cosmos, and Islamic prophetology. It also contains a summary of Ṣadrā's political philosophy and his views on the role of the prophets in religion, miracles, the difference between revelation (*waḥy*) and intuition (*ilhām*), politics, and the aims of the Divine Law (*al-Sharīʿa*). *Ḥuduth al-ʿālam* (Temporal Origination of the World) is Ṣadrā's most important work on this theme – one that he considers essential for the unity of philosophical and revealed forms of knowledge.

Eschatology is of particular relevance for the Transcendent Wisdom because it extends the great chain of being into the hereafter and invites us to contemplate the final stages of the journey of the human state and the universe. While the *Asfār* deals with the afterlife and resurrection, *al-Ḥikmat al-ʿarshiyya* (The Wisdom of the Throne) is a major work on eschatology in which Ṣadrā has applied the principles of his philosophy to eschatological questions. A similar yet shorter work is *Risālat al-Ḥashr* (Treatise on the Resurrection). In his eschatological works, Ṣadrā bases his analyses on the Qurʾān and defends the resurrection of all existence, including the animal and plant kingdoms and the mineral world. In tandem with his ontology and natural philosophy, which considers the world of creation to be various degrees and modes of the all-inclusive reality of existence through ontological gradation, Ṣadrā provides a fairly detailed description of the return of the great chain of being to its point of origin. It is also in these works that Ṣadrā defends the thesis that the entire world of existence including material bodies is alive and has consciousness by virtue of the fact that they share, no matter how small or low, a degree of existence.

Finally, Ṣadrā has written several works on Sufism. *Iksīr al-ʿārifīn fī maʿrifa ṭarīq al-ḥaqq wa-l-yaqīn* (The Elixir of the Gnostics for Knowing the Path of the Truth and Certainty) treats the question of knowledge from a Sufi point of view and discusses the human soul as the recipient of all knowledge, man's ability to know, the end of all knowledge, and the ultimate return of things to God. *Īqāẓ al-nāʾimīn* (Awakening the Sleepers) shows how a proper understanding of ontology and epistemology in the Ṣadrean sense leads to realized knowledge and spiritual refinement. The *Īqāẓ* is also a gem of philosophical insights and spiritual exhortations. *Kasr al-aṣnām al-jāhiliyya fī dhamm al-mutaṣawwifīn* (The Demolition of the Idols of Ignorance in Blaming the Pseudo-Sufis) is a critique of ignorant ascetics who claim to be masters of spiritual knowledge. But it is also an eloquent exposition of the meaning of Divine knowledge and how the reciprocity between realized knowledge (*maʿrifa*) and spiritual practice (*riyāḍa*) leads to virtue and perfection.

2

The intellectual journey of a seventeenth-century Muslim philosopher

Mullā Ṣadrā flourished at a critical juncture in Islamic intellectual history. He emerged as a young student of philosophy against the backdrop of a well-established philosophical tradition. He worked within that tradition and also challenged and reworked its key premises. By the end of the sixteenth century, the three basic perspectives of *kalām*, Peripatetic philosophy and doctrinal Sufism had already developed into major schools of thought with wide-ranging areas of overlap and criss-crossing. Each had developed a distinct method of enquiry and, in some cases, a somewhat independent set of issues. The fundamental questions of metaphysics, however, were shared by all: the problem of existence and non-existence, the relation between the Creator and the created, unity and multiplicity, causality, and evil, happiness and the ultimate goal of human existence on earth were among the common philosophical issues that connected the various strands of the Islamic intellectual tradition.

When Ṣadrā began his philosophical career in Isfahan, the political and religious landscape of Safavid Iran had been shaped to a large extent by the process of *tashayyuʿ*, i.e., establishing Twelve Imam Shiʿism as the official religious code of Iran, begun in the early 1500s by Shāh Ismāʿīl, the founder of the Safavid dynasty. This process, while having its own dynamics, was closely linked to the long-standing political rivalry between the Ottomans and the Safavids. Having emerged in fourteenth-century western Anatolia, the Ottomans expanded into western Thrace, gradually subsumed other frontier states around them and conquered Istanbul in 1453. This watershed event, the dream of many Muslim commanders for centuries, turned the Ottoman state into the most powerful political force by the second half of the fifteenth century. In the sixteenth and seventeenth centuries, the Ottoman Empire became the political leader of much of the Sunni world and ruled over a vast territory from the Balkans and Western Thrace to North Africa and the present-day Middle East. A major confrontation between the powerful Ottomans and the newly founded Safavid dynasty was inevitable for both religious and political reasons.

Founded by Shāh Ismāʿīl I in 1501, the Safavids had their origins in Safawiyya, a Sunni Sufi order founded by Ṣafī al-Dīn Ardabīlī (d. 1334). In the latter part of the fifteenth century, the Safawiyya spread among various tribes in eastern Anatolia and western Iran. Among those were what the Ottomans called the '*qizilbash*', 'the red-heads', referring to the red headgear they wore to express their loyalty to the Safawiyya. When Shāh Ismāʿīl I declared himself the leader of the Qizilbash, he also announced Twelve-Imam Shiʿism as the official sect of the Safawiyya order. Fearing religious dissent and political disloyalty, the Ottomans were quick to respond and scored a decisive victory against Shāh Ismāʿīl in the battle of Chaldiran, near Khoi, in 1514. The defeat was devastating for Shāh Ismāʿīl's political career and he never reclaimed his authority over the various tribal leaders loyal to him before.

When Shāh Ismāʿīl died in 1524, however, the *tashayyuʿ* policy which he had instituted had largely succeeded in turning much of present-day Persia into a Shiʿi country. This forced such Sunni Sufi orders as the Naqshbandiyya, Khalwatiyya, Nurbakhshiyya, Niʿmatullahiyya and the Qalandariyya-Malamatiyya out of the territories under Safavid rule. As a result, prominent Sufi orders migrated and found home in adjacent regions from the Ottoman Empire and Mesopotamia to the subcontinent of India.

Mullā Ṣadrā lived during the reigns of Muḥammad Khudābanda (1578–87), Shāh ʿAbbās I (1587–1629), and Shāh Ṣafī (1629–42). These rulers, much like their predecessors and successors, had the same socio-political agenda: consolidating the internal unity of their subjects, securing the borders of the state against the Ottomans and other smaller forces, encouraging trade with India and Europe, cultivating the arts and sciences in Persian cities, and spreading Twelve-Imam Shiʿism in the Safavid territories. This was coupled with the rise of Shiʿi ulema as the ultimate source of religious authority among the Safavid Shiʿis. The three cities of Shiraz, Qazvin and Isfahan, in which Ṣadrā was born, flourished and composed his works, carried the characteristics of a new sense of political identity, religious commitment, intellectual and artistic competition, and economic prosperity. The political and military rivalry between the Ottomans and Safavids seems to have prevented much of the social and economic activity that could have developed between the two states. Despite the political and sectarian hostilities, however, the philosophical and spiritual sources that nourished the Ottoman and Safavid intellectual and artistic worlds have maintained a degree of commonality across the Sunni and Shiʿi circles from the Balkans to the subcontinent of India.

SUFISM AND SHIʿISM

The rise of a distinctively Shiʿi spirituality with a vocabulary taken mostly from Sunni Sufis such as Ibn ʿArabī and his followers Ṣadr al-Dīn al-Qūnawī and Dāwūd al-Qayṣarī is interesting and intriguing. While connection with Shiʿi Imams has always had a spiritual-mystical dimension, a fully developed Shiʿi Sufism would emerge after the fourteenth century and quickly become an underlying current in the work of Persian-Shiʿi theologians and philosophers including our own Ṣadrā. Just as the school of Ibn ʿArabī, with its profound and challenging philosophical ideas, closed the gap between philosophy and Sufism in the Sunni world, Twelve Imam Shiʿism and Sufism began to display a rapprochement both unexpected and with far-reaching consequences for later Islamic thought. A key figure for the formulation of a sophisticated Shiʿi Sufism with clear references to the school of Ibn ʿArabī was Ḥaydar Āmulī (d. *ca.* 1385). An intellectual follower of Ibn ʿArabī and a first-rate philosophical mind, Āmulī restated the fundamental teachings of Shiʿism and Akbarian Sufism in terms of a shared metaphysical framework and made the daring claim that a true Shiʿi, someone who has reached the level of what he called the 'tested believer', cannot but be a Sufi and a true Sufi who has understood the secrets of *tawḥīd*, Divine Unity, cannot but be a follower of the Shiʿi Imams. In his *Jāmiʿ al-asrār wa-manbaʿ al-anwār* and other equally important works, Āmulī tried to show the underlying unity between Shiʿi spirituality and Sufi metaphysics, and introduced Ibn ʿArabī into the Persian Shiʿi philosophical world in such a way that Ibn ʿArabī and his teachings became and have remained to this day an integral part of the Persian intellectual scene. Āmulī also attempted to overcome the historical divide between the Sunni and Shiʿi worlds – a divide that eventually disappeared in the domains of philosophy, metaphysics and spirituality.

However, this introduction of Sufism into Shiʿism, through the most metaphysical and philosophical school of all Sufism, had another unexpected outcome, and this was the development of a distinction between what is called 'theoretical Sufism' (*ʿirfān-i naẓarī*) and 'practical Sufism' (*ʿirfān-i ʿamalī*). Coupled with the particular nature of Twelve Imam Shiʿism as an integral path of both faith and spiritual wayfaring, the distinction came to state and justify the separation of the study of the metaphysical teachings of Sufism from following a particular Sufi order – a conclusion that most Sufi orders would find suspect, even dangerous. Given the specific historical experience of Safavid Shiʿism, this outcome was somewhat inevitable because the Safavid rulers and religious authorities did not trust the political loyalty and religious allegiance of Sunni Sufi orders. But they did not want to throw the baby out with the bath-water and allowed the higher metaphysical ideas of Sufism to flourish. Furthermore, it was relatively easy to jettison the central role of the Sufi master in view of the overall mission and personality of the Shiʿi Imam who was the religious, spiritual, doctrinal, social and juridical source of authority all at once. It was generally accepted that, if a devout Shiʿi wants to follow the spiritual path, he or she can do so by connecting with the Imam without necessarily following a Sufi master.

Within this new framework, it was by and large assumed that one could study Sufism without necessarily following a Sufi master and entering a particular order. Traditional Sufism, however, stipulates that there is no spiritual path without following a master, and even such exceptions as the ʿUwaysis who have become major spiritual personalities without earthly masters have their spiritual lineage go back to a prophet or a great saint. Since most Sufis have been historically Sunnis, the distinction between the theory and practice of Sufism has allowed Shiʿi thinkers and philosophers to study the metaphysical teachings of the Sufis without compromising the tenets of Shiʿi Islam. This does not mean that there are no Shiʿi Sufi orders. As a matter of fact, such orders as the Kubrawiyya and Nurbakhshiyya have survived in Iran with Shiʿi followings and developed their own particular style and code of conduct. The difficult relationship between Shiʿism and organized Sufism, however, ended up forcing most of the Sufi orders out of Iran, leaving a space for Sufi ideas largely under the rubric of *ʿirfān-i naẓarī*.

Ṣadrā flourished in a milieu which witnessed the convergence of various philosophical, intellectual and religious strands in Persia. Even though Shiʿism had become the dominant religious identity of most Persians by the end of the sixteenth century, different intellectual currents continued to live within Safavid Shiʿism.

Four major schools of thought influenced scores of thinkers in Persia including Mullā Ṣadrā: the Peripatetic philosophy represented by al-Fārābī and Ibn Sīnā; the School of Illumination (*ishrāq*) founded by Shihāb al-Dīn Suhrawardī al-Maqtūl; Ibn ʿArabī and his students Ṣadr al-Dīn al-Qūnawī and Dāʾūd al-Qayṣarī; and Sunni and Shiʿi *kalām* debates. These were all instrumental in the creation of a new philosophical synthesis that would find its finest expression in Ṣadrā's 'Transcendent Wisdom'. Ṣadrā's honorific titles (as discussed above), Akhund, Ṣadr al-Dīn, and Ṣadr al-Mutaʾallihīn, attest to his ability to combine these diverse perspectives and strands into a unified philosophical vision. But no master is born without the hand of another, and Ṣadrā studied under two towering figures of his time.

IN THE PRESENCE OF THE TWO MASTERS

Ṣadrā's two main teachers were Sayyid Bāqir Muḥammad Astarābādī, known as Mīr Dāmād (d. 1040/1631) and Bahāʾ al-Dīn Muḥammad al-ʿĀmilī known more popularly as Shaykh Bahāʾī (d. 1031/1622). Shaykh Bahāʾī was one of the most prominent scholars of his time. He was a polymath: at once a philosopher, theologian, jurist, mathematician, architect, Sufi, poet, anthologist, and traveller. Originally from Lebanon, Shaykh Bahāʾī belonged to a family of prominent scholars and migrated to Qazwin, the capital of the Safavid Empire at the time, where he quickly became one of the most recognized and respected scholars of his era. His disregard for worldly wealth and his quest for spirituality combined with his mastery of Sufism gained him the reputation of a saintly person. As a major scholar and guide, he was an inclusivist and embraced diverse points of view, whether philosophical or spiritual, Shiʿi or Sunni. This explains why some later sources refer to him as a Sunni even though he was clearly a follower of Twelve Imam Shiʿism.

Shaykh Bahāʾī was a prolific writer. He composed some ninety works in such diverse disciplines as Qurʾānic commentary, hadith, jurisprudence, mathematics, astronomy and Arabic language and literature. He also authored several works in Persian. *Al-Kashkūl*, his most famous book in the Arabic-speaking world, is an anthology of wisdom sayings and literary expressions and has been translated into several languages.

The fact that the manuscripts of his books are found in many libraries from Istanbul to Tehran and India attests to his widespread influence and popularity. In addition, Shaykh Bahāʾī was known for his travels around the Muslim world as a dervish, especially in Egypt, Iraq, the Hijaz, Syria and Turkey.

Ṣadrā's master in the intellectual-philosophical sciences was Sayyid Bāqir Muḥammad Astarābādī known more commonly as Mīr 'Dāmād', meaning the 'son-in-law' because his father Mīr Shams al-Dīn was married to the daughter of ʿAlī ibn Ḥusayn al-Karakī, the pre-eminent Shiʿi cleric of the Safavids. Mīr Dāmād was a towering figure of his time and became famous, just like Shaykh Bahāʾī, for his sharp mind, scholarly erudition and spiritual life. Representing the maturity of intellectual sciences in later Islamic history, Mīr Dāmād was recognized as an authority in the Qurʾānic sciences, hadith, jurisprudence, medicine, mathematics, linguistics and philosophy all at once. As a prolific writer, he composed some fifty works, many of them still unedited and unpublished. His students acknowledged his prominence by giving him the honorific title 'Third Teacher' after Aristotle the 'first teacher' and al-Fārābī the 'second teacher'. He had such a major influence already during his lifetime that some modern scholars have credited him with founding the 'School of Isfahan' in Islamic philosophy.

It is clear from Ṣadrā's autobiographical notes and letters that he had a special relationship with Mīr Dāmād. A scholastic teacher and a spiritual mentor at once, Mīr Dāmād left an enduring mark on Ṣadrā's intellectual upbringing and spiritual quest. Ṣadrā acknowledges his debt to his master on various occasions and accords him such honorific titles as 'the eleventh intellect, the container of the details and principles [of true knowledge], the noble prince, the prince of the philosophers, the master of the jurists, the supreme teacher of the teachers and scholars, the most noble of the nobles...' Ṣadrā's affection for his teacher was reciprocated by Mīr Dāmād who called Ṣadrā 'a spiritual son and the closest person to have an intellectual relationship [with him]'.

Mīr Dāmād's influence on Ṣadrā was so heavy that the disciple would become an ardent proponent of his master's teachings, including the key Ishraqi doctrine that what is real and fundamental in beings is their essence rather than existence. This question, lying at the heart of Ṣadrā's attempt to formulate a metaphysical system based on the absolute unity and centrality of existence, would eventually lead him to part ways with his mentor. Following in the footsteps of Suhrawardī, Mīr Dāmād had established essence as the fundamental reality of things and reduced existence to a common attribute or predicate, which adds nothing to and extracts nothing from the actual reality of things. In his *al-Qabasāt ḥaqq al-yaqīn fī ḥuduth al-ʿālam* (Firebrands: the Certain Truth concerning the Temporal Origination of the World), his great work of philosophy, Mīr Dāmād mobilizes all of his intellectual genius and erudition to construct an essence-based metaphysics.

CHARTING A NEW WAY

Ṣadrā was destined to confront his teacher on the most fundamental of all metaphysical issues, i.e., the primacy of existence, and he took a position that put him squarely in opposition to Mīr Dāmād, who had devoted a good part of his philosophical career, with commendable force and consistency, to the defence of the primacy of essence. It was this intellectual revolt that turned Ṣadrā into who he became.

Ṣadrā describes this awakening in vivid terms:

... In the days gone by I was a vigorous defender of the thesis of the principiality of quiddities and the conceptuality of *wujūd* until my Lord guided me and made me see its proof. Then it was unveiled to me with supreme evidence that [the case of the quiddities] was the reverse of what they conceived and decided [concerning this matter]. Glory be to God Who through the light of veritable understanding allowed me to leave the darkness of opinion, who made the clouds of doubt in my heart dissipate through the rising of the Sun of the Truth, and who established me on the 'firm doctrine' in this life and in the hereafter. Existences are the principial realities, whereas quiddities are the 'fixed essences' (*al-aᶜyān al-thābita*) which have never smelled the perfume of real existence. And [these] existences are none other than the rays and gleamings of the Light of Truth and the Eternal, exalted be His sublimeness. (*Mashāᶜir*, §85)

Though Ṣadrā parted ways with Mīr Dāmād and the Ishraqi tradition by arguing for the primacy of existence, he nevertheless adopted many of his teachers' ideas. Among Mīr Dāmād's enduring contributions to philosophy and one that engaged Ṣadrā extensively is the highly original concept Mīr Dāmād called 'the temporal origination of the world' (*al-ḥudūth al-dahrī*). Taking up the perennial problem of the creation of the world, Mīr Dāmād sought to establish, in contrast to the Peripatetic philosophers, that the world is created not only 'essentially' but also 'temporally', i.e., 'in time' as we understand the term. The Peripatetic idea that the world is created by God but co-eternal with Him was an inevitable result of the Aristotelian metaphysics of fixed substances. This conclusion was troubling, to say the least, for the Muslim philosophers because it assumed something to be co-terminate with God. A created being cannot be eternal, and only God can be both eternal and creating. One needs, then, to develop a concept of time and creation that can explain how God has created things both essentially and temporally, i.e., at a particular point before which they did not exist. Having seen the dichotomies of Peripatetic metaphysics for the creation of the world, Ṣadrā tried to defend the essential and temporal origination of the world as a key component of his Transcendent Wisdom.

Here, we may briefly mention another important, rather enigmatic figure of the period, Mīr Abū l-Qāṣim Findiriskī (d. *ca.* 1050/1640–1). He appears to have been one of the most interesting personalities of the Safavid cultural renaissance in the early seventeenth century. Judging by his extant works, one can call Mīr Findiriskī a follower of Ibn Sīnā. Indeed, he taught Ibn Sīnā's works in his classes. Mīr Findiriskī, however, was not a Peripatetic philosopher in the ordinary sense of the term. In addition to his wide interests in logic, philosophy, natural sciences and anthropology, he was also a spiritual traveller. He was famous for shunning and ridiculing the world and its pleasures. His interest in Sufism had a universalist dimension, which eventually led him to travel to India where he is reported to have met a number of Hindu sages and ascetics. One of the fruits of these travels was his Persian commentary on the Hindu mystical and philosophical text *Yoga-Vasishtha*. This commentary is an important text from the point of view of both comparative philosophy and cultural history under the Safavids. Some sources add Mīr Findiriskī to the list of masters with whom Ṣadrā studied in Isfahan but no compelling evidence has been provided in support of this claim.

Mīr Findiriskī complements Shaykh Bahāʾī's legal personality and Mīr Dāmād's sharp analytic mind. In these three figures, we have a near perfect composite of the Islamic tradition: law, philosophy and wisdom. Law sets boundaries for individual and collective behaviour; philosophy teaches how to think properly; and wisdom leads to moral perfection and spiritual refinement – the ultimate goal of all knowledge and asceticism. Each of these three corresponds in its own way to essential aspects of an ideal Muslim life; together, they show the unity of human existence – an intellectual and spiritual unity which Ṣadrā sought to achieve in his own way.

THE QUESTION OF 'METHOD'

Ṣadrā worked from within a rich tradition of different schools of thought which had developed over the centuries. Indeed, he regarded this diversity as an asset, not a deficit, which served to deepen his thinking. From the transmitted-religious sciences to the natural and intellectual sciences, previous Muslim scholars had dealt with a large number of issues and produced solutions with divergent points of view. Ṣadrā was intimately aware of these differences and believed that they could be brought under a unifying philosophical vision. Transcendent Wisdom seeks to accomplish this task.

Ṣadrā was a 'unifier': he wanted to synthesize the major strands of the Islamic intellectual tradition and refused to sacrifice any one of them. His wide ranging interests in traditional religious sciences, classical Sunni and Shiʿi theology, Peripatetic philosophy, the school of Illumination, Sufi metaphysics and spiritual anthropology, point to Ṣadrā's genuine concern to embrace the entire spectrum of Islamic thought. At times, he appears just to be faithfully reporting previous discussions on a particular issue. This is extremely valuable because it allows us to see how Ṣadrā read the history of philosophy. His main interest in history was two-fold: to understand the 'life of the mind' as it developed in history, and to articulate a vision of reality which embraced and transcended history.

In order to achieve his synthesis, Ṣadrā applies a vertical rather than horizontal arrangement. Instead of juxtaposing the perspectives of, say, jurists, philosophers or Platonists and looking for a common denominator among their views, he places them in a hierarchical order and examines where each of them belongs in the overall scheme of things. The juridical perspective is correct at its level of analysis but may be misleading if applied to a domain of knowledge beyond its competencies. A Peripatetic approach may be useful and even necessary to understanding a logical or discursive problem but cannot be applied as-is to a domain of metaphysics that requires a different kind of epistemology. Similarly, the specific experiences of the visionary mystic cannot be used to understand a mathematical problem, which requires a different set of premises and instruments.

Ṣadrā sees no necessary contradiction between these different levels of analysis because the order of being is structured hierarchically and for each degree of existence there is an epistemology proper to it. It is a philosophical mistake to reduce the multiple states of being to one, as literalists seek to do, or to confound them as some pretentious ascetics do. In the first case, we end up with ontological reductionism and epistemic rigidity. In the latter, we run into syncretism and cannot understand the reality of things in their proper context.

Ṣadrā respects each perspective and framework of analysis at its own level and tries to show that each makes sense when all are seen in a hierarchical arrangement. A physicist can study minerals and plants by employing his five senses. A logician can establish connections between propositions by using his reason. A mystic can speak of the intuition of existence by having a vision of the truth. Ṣadrā sees no contradiction between these different modes of analysis because each corresponds to a different state of existence. However, when Ṣadrā speaks of degrees of knowledge and understanding, he has in mind not just different methods but also different degrees of existence because, as we shall see, knowledge is ultimately nothing but a modality of existence. Transcendent Wisdom begins with this fundamental insight and works its way through the rich alleys of traditional philosophy.

REASON AND THREE TYPES OF KNOWLEDGE

Ṣadrā's lifelong quest to show the unity of rational-demonstrative knowledge and intuitive-mystical vision under the guidance of revealed knowledge is a natural result of this insight. In his introduction to *Mafātiḥ al-ghayb*, a profound work of Qurʾānic hermeneutics and philosophical reflection, Ṣadrā defines this as a unitary vision of *qurʾān*, *ʿirfān* and *burhān* and says that the proper study of the Qurʾān leads to the 'unveiling of the marvels of the fundamental issues of *ʿirfān* and brings together wisdom and demonstration' (*Mafātiḥ*, i. 77). *Burhān* refers to logical and philosophical argumentation and covers human knowledge as it applies to the logical and scientific nature of things. It ensures that we understand correctly the relation between concept and reality on the one hand, and between concepts on the other. There is no proper human thinking without *burhān*. *ʿIrfān*, 'gnosis' or realized knowledge, can be attained only through spiritual training and purification of the soul. Finally, *qurʾān* refers to revealed knowledge as the principal source of truth that transcends other forms of knowledge. It is the source of the knowledge of God, which is the penultimate goal of all philosophy and reflection. A true philosopher and sage must have all three. The truth of what is essential can be attained only 'through the light of prophecy and sainthood', which suggests that the knowing mind can know the truth but cannot claim to be its sole proprietor (*Tafsīr*, vii. 10).

Lest we think these three are separate from one another, it should be stressed that there is an underlying relationship between them and each stimulates something in the other. The Qurʾān urges its readers to use their reason and see God's wisdom and mercy in His creation. Gnosis is not without cognitive content and a true sage can explain his vision by using ordinary rational arguments. Furthermore, philosophical-discursive thinking is not a goal in itself. A real philosophy, based on the truth which empowers and overpowers, urges us to go beyond the confines of logical demonstration and invites us to the non-discursive, meta-philosophical world. Ṣadrā often states that 'true demonstration (*al-burhān al-ḥaqīqī*) does not contradict witnessing based on unveiling (*al-shuhūd al-kashfī*)' (*Asfār*, i. 2. 315). In tandem with his gnostic viewpoint, Ṣadrā understands demonstration in terms of sound proof and irrefutable evidence whether it comes from logical reasoning or mystical experience. In *Kasr aṣnām al-jāhiliyya*, he quotes Ḥallāj's definition of *burhān* to underscore this point: 'It is what descends upon the heart which the souls are incapable of denying' (*Kasr*, 13).

It is within this context that we should understand Ṣadrā's supreme confidence in 'reason' or 'intellect'. Human reason is a divine gift revealing the truth and guiding us in our moral choices: 'reason... is one of the words of God and... does not change in its true judgment of the plurality of existing beings insofar as its original, pure nature is concerned' (*Asfār*, i.

2. 322). In its 'original, pure nature', reason is a bliss, a light which enlightens our path and brings out the best in us, i.e., our humanity as it moves to its final *telos*. Ṣadrā places human reason within a larger context of meaning and intelligibility:

ʿAyn al-Quḍāt Hamadhānī said in [his] *Zubdat [al-ḥaqāʾiq]*: 'Know that reason is a true scale and its judgments are true and certain with no lies. It is just from which no injustice is to be expected.' It is clear from the statement of these two Masters [Ghazālī and Hamadhānī] that there is no error in the judgment of true reason. How then can great people like them who are detached from the material garment of humanity with their spiritual asceticism and struggle say something which a fair judge, i.e., true reason, finds to be impossible? The truth is that whoever has a deep step in Sufism and gnosis does not deny the existence of contingent beings with his head [i.e., reason]. (*Asfār*, i. 2. 323)

On account of its innate ability and ontological status, reason is not separable from the truth of existence. It can thus discover the reality of things. But it deviates when it begins to see itself as the sole arbiter of truth. Ṣadrā never tires of warning against this temptation and insists on the hierarchy of the multiple modes of knowing and gives autobiographical examples from his own experience.

I used to busy myself with investigation (*al-baḥth*) and repetition, referring constantly to the study of the books of the philosophers of theory so much so that I believed that I had gained something. When my vision began to open a little bit and I looked at myself... [and saw that I was] far from having the knowledge of the truths and the real truths, which cannot be perceived except through tasting (*dhawq*) and consciousness (*wijdān*). These are explained in the Book [i.e., the Qurʾān] and the Sunna concerning the knowledge of God, His attributes and names, books, prophets, and the knowledge of the soul and its states in the grave, the resurrection, the reckoning, the scale, the bridge, and the heaven and hellfire, whose truth cannot be known except through the teaching of God and cannot be unveiled except through the light of prophethood and sanctity. (*Tafsīr*, vii. 10)

In the *Īqāẓ*, he says that he has discussed Divine Unity according to the methods and arguments of discursive philosophy because this is what 'most scholars..., philosophers and the virtuous [thinkers] have accepted... what I mention in this book is a different, divine method and a new sacred style which only the true knower of divine unity can appreciate...' (*Īqāẓ*, 7).

While the human mind can grasp the essential properties of the world of existence and bring out its meaning, reality evades conceptualization. All rationalist and empiricist attempts to reduce reality to human epistemic competencies fail to give a proper account of it as a whole. One needs different methods and ways of knowing the multilayered and multidimensional nature of reality. Thus Ṣadrā says: 'the knowledge of what is tasted and the knowledge of spiritual states cannot be properly captured in the garment of letters and words. Whoever has not tasted has not known' (*Īqāẓ*, 8).

The unity of the multiple ways of knowing is a reflection of the underlying unity of reality itself. When scientists study the universe, they study its physical properties not as an end in itself but as part of a larger whole. The larger context of intelligibility provided by the all-encompassing reality of existence brings out the intellectual principles in the universe. It is these principles which first and foremost concern the philosopher. Corporeal beings are a manifestation of existence at the lowest form of reality; what really deserves the attention of the philosopher is the principles behind them. Existence, which is the ultimate source of all beings and their meanings, is best understood in the form of universal principles. Ṣadrā sums up this point in the following paragraph, explaining at the same time the perennial task of the philosopher:

Every celestial or elemental nature has an intellective substance as its principle and a substance that changes its existence. The relation of this intellective substance to these corporeal natures is like the relation of the perfect to the imperfect and of the principle to the derivative. God is ever closer to us than anything else, and these intellective substances are like the lights and rays of the First Necessary Light, for they are the forms of what is in God's knowledge. Furthermore, they do not have an independent existence by themselves; their very essence is related to the Truth. (*Asfār*, i. 3. 95–6)

In his autobiographical essay, Ṣadrā states that, after studying metaphysics and mastering the views of the previous philosophers and 'whatever I was able to find in the books of the Greeks' (*Asfār*, i. 1. 4), he was confronted with the adverse attitude of some 'simple-minded scholars', i.e., the Akhbārīs, whom Ṣadrā compares to the Sunni Hanbali scholars of hadith, known in Islamic history for their strict literalism and anti-intellectualism. He does not mince his words when condemning the feeble-mindedness of such people and admonishes them for failing to understand the 'Transcendent Wisdom' (*Asfār*, i. 1. 6). These exotericists-literalists also fail to grasp the true meaning of revelation and spiritual realization. 'A group has emerged in our age', complains Ṣadrā, 'who see deep penetration into divine sciences and meditating upon the Lord's verses as innovation and sin'. While they count both reason and piety among the resources of their thinking, they touch only the surface of things and cannot go beyond the 'the world of darkness'. Ṣadrā uses very strong language against these pretentious jurists and ascetics and even quotes the following verse to describe their blindness: 'They have hearts with which they do not understand, they have eyes with which they do not see, and they have ears with which they do not hear. Those are like livestock; rather, they are more astray. It is they who are the heedless.' (*al-Aʿrāf*, 7: 179; *Mafātiḥ*, i. 77–8). These simplistic and arrogant ascetics-cum-scholars confuse the true seekers of knowledge. More disturbingly, they accuse others of innovation and deviation. Ṣadrā counsels his followers simply to ignore these 'pretentious Sufis' (*al-mutaṣawwifa*) and 'pretentious philosophers' (*al-mutafalsifa*) (*Mafātiḥ*, i. 80).

THE MEANING AND FUNCTION OF PHILOSOPHY

Ṣadrā takes philosophy as a full-scale enterprise and as a way of life. His treatment of the role and meaning of philosophy is comparable to Abū Bakr al-Rāzī's 'philosophical life'. Both philosophers agree that philosophy is more than mental gymnastics and that the search for the truth touches our whole existence. The difference is that Rāzī seems to be content with good philosophy whereas Ṣadrā sees philosophy like Wittgenstein's ladder: when you climb the wall, you throw away the ladder and move on. A philosophical doctrine that does not lead to the total transformation of the seeker of knowledge does not have much meaning. Philosophy as 'the art of spiritual dying' should teach us how to die so that we can be reborn spiritually. This is where philosophy becomes a 'spiritual exercise', a 'conversion' that takes us beyond our individual thoughts and desires and grounds us in existence. The goal of philosophical quest is to transform our whole being and transcend our individual existence within the 'horizon of being', to use Ṣadrā's suggestive term. While the philosopher does justice to the minute details of the arguments at hand, what matters essentially is the intellectual-spiritual journey which the seeker of knowledge takes. This is not simply conceptual knowledge combined with ethics. The nature of the journey is such that each act of learning and un-learning corresponds to an aspect of reality and brings us closer to the universal purview of being.

To underscore this meaning of philosophy, Ṣadrā relates everything to the all-inclusive reality of existence. But he also goes back to history to show that a single, continuous tradition of philosophy-cum-spiritual exercise has lived on unabated. He thus quotes some sages as saying that 'whoever wants divine wisdom, he should create a new nature for himself'. Plato urged his students 'to die voluntarily so that we can live naturally [i.e., with a new nature]'. Jesus Christ is reported to have said that 'the sacred dominion of the heavens will never let in a person who is not born twice'. The Prophet of Islam has said 'to die before you die', meaning that we must die to worldly desires so that we can be reborn spiritually before we depart this world. Finally, Ṣadrā quotes Imam ʿAlī: 'People are asleep; they wake up when they die' (*Mafātiḥ*, i. 81).

The interplay between logical demonstration and spiritual realization informs Ṣadrā's philosophical quest. It also explains his personal journey through the stages of human knowledge and moral perfection. His refraining from political life and from the machinations of worldly scholars is both a personal and philosophical choice. By concentrating on the Truth alone, Ṣadrā protected himself from the human frailties and moral failures around him. But by doing so, he also attained a degree of intellectual and spiritual perfection that shaped his new school of thought:

I restrained my thoughts from dealing with people and mixing with them, and abstained from their companionship and friendship. Then the turning of cycles [i.e., the passing of days] and the obstinacy of the people of the present time became easier for me. I released myself from their repudiation and acceptance, and their praise and harm became equal for me. Then I turned my face to the Cause of all causes, and humbled myself before the One who makes all difficult matters easy. I stayed in this state of secrecy, retreat, obscurity, and withdrawal for a long time. I busied myself with long moments of spiritual exercise as a luminous work, and my heart burned with the desire of attaining more spiritual discipline in a very strong way. Then the lights of the angelic world began to emanate upon my heart, the secrets of the world of Dominion (*jabarūt*) were unfolded, the light of the One reached it, the Divine subtleties came upon it, and I obtained the secrets of which I was not aware before. The symbols were unveiled to me, and this unveiling was not a result of logical demonstration. On the contrary, with a plenitude of direct witnessing and seeing of the Divine mysteries, I witnessed everything that I had learned before through logical demonstration.' (*Asfār*, i. 1. 7–8)

3

Crisis and maturity: introducing Ṣadrā's ontology

Ṣadrā called his school of philosophy 'Transcendent Wisdom' (*al-ḥikmat al-mutaʿāliya*). Even though variants of this term had been used by Ibn Sīnā, Dāwūd al-Qaysarī and others before him, Ṣadrā's use of it signifies the new philosophical outlook that he sought to create out of the various strands of the Islamic intellectual tradition. His thinking is a response to what he saw as a crisis in Islamic philosophy, namely the gradual disappearance of 'existence' (*al-wujūd*) as the ground of philosophical and theological thinking and the emergence of schools of thought that claimed to explain reality with, on the one hand, the epistemic and psychological competencies of the human mind and with, on the other, a firm belief in God. The Peripatetic tradition failed to explain fully the relation between reason and existence and treated the latter mostly as a conceptual tool, mistaking the *concept* of existence for its *reality*. Most *mutakallimūn* took comfort in pietistic theology and ended up with different versions of fideism in the name of safeguarding orthodoxy.

According to Ṣadrā, the theologians did not realize that a meaningful theology is not possible without a proper metaphysics and ontology. Defending faith at the expense of rational argument is not in conformity with the spirit of the Qurʾān which urges its readers to use their reason to understand the reality of things and God. Furthermore, it is wrong to reduce philosophy to what the Peripatetics had made out of it and then reject it as irrelevant or impious. Finally, most Sufis have had a long pendulum moment between mysticism without sound philosophical basis on the one hand, and asceticism without metaphysics on the other. As a result, philosophy became a soulless mental exercise, theology the art of dialectical bickering, and Sufism ascetic practice without intellectual content.

THE CRISIS OF EPISTEMOLOGY

The crisis of fundamental metaphysics was coupled with another crisis in epistemology. Simply put, this was the problem of what constitutes veritable knowledge – the kind of knowledge that is based on logical-rational argument on the one hand, and intuition and spiritual realization on the other. Moreover, in the Islamic context, there was also the Qurʾān as Divine revelation, which as a form of knowledge pertained to other types of knowing and moral-spiritual perfection. For Ṣadrā, the crisis of Muslim epistemology resulted from a failure to respect the different types of knowledge and to establish a harmonious and integrated relationship between them.

Aristotle's Muslim followers were content with the promise of their rational outlook and treated non-discursive types of knowledge as irrelevant to the primary task of philosophy. They constructed a conceptual edifice based on logical proofs and philosophical demonstration. Their system of thought, however, contained certain anomalies that eventually led to serious philosophical-cum-theological problems especially in regard to such issues as God's interaction with the created order, the eternity of the world, the nature of revelation, and the representational theory of knowledge. The theologians' concept of knowledge, Ṣadrā believed, was largely subjectivist and instrumentalist, lacking sound foundation in either pure rational demonstration or intuitive cognition. As for the Sufis, with notable exceptions such as Ibn ʿArabī and his followers, most of them neglected the intellectual foundation of their spiritual experience and took an adverse position against philosophical reflection. By Ṣadrā's time, much of the serious intellectual activity in the Muslim world seemed to have been divided between dry discursive thinking without spiritual content and religious devotion without intellectual content. For Ṣadrā, both perspectives were flawed and failed to ensure the unity and integrity of knowing and experiencing.

Before Ṣadrā, Suhrawardī, the founder of the school of 'Illumination' (*ishrāq*), was aware of this crisis in epistemology and sought to overcome it by engaging both the Peripatetic and Sufi traditions. He introduced and elaborated the concept of 'knowledge by presence' (*al-ʿilm al-ḥuḍūrī*) to explain the types of knowledge that went beyond 'acquired knowledge' (*al-ʿilm al-ḥuṣūlī*) based solely on empirical evidence and rational argument. The Master of Illumination held that true knowledge comes about not only through empirical and rational methods but also through illumination, unveiling, clearing and presence. Knowledge as 'unveiling' and 'clearing', Suhrawardī held, is a result of a direct and unmediated encounter with the reality of things, i.e., their essence. This is the basis of the notion of 'knowledge by presence' and opens up a new chapter in the history of Islamic epistemology. Ṣadrā largely concurred with Suhrawardī on the necessity of 'knowledge by presence' for metaphysics and took up his unfinished work to establish mystical knowledge as sound and veritable. But Ṣadrā was also aware of Suhrawardī's ontology of radical essentialism and criticized him for not seeing the connection between existence and knowledge – a connection of whose importance Ṣadrā never tires of reminding us.

He replaced Suhrawardī's 'essence' with existence and turned essence and all related concepts into a subcategory of existence. Before he was able to do this, Ṣadrā himself went through a philosophical crisis. He had begun his philosophical career under Mīr Dāmād and followed his master's essentialist metaphysics, a legacy of the School of Illumination, which held (much as would Kant in the eighteenth century) that existence is a mental concept and does not furnish us with any new knowledge about the reality of things. Existence is a general property shared by all existing beings and cannot be the basis of their reality. As such, it is not relevant to philosophical metaphysics except in a secondary manner. 'Essence' makes things what they are and should be the main concern of philosophical analysis. In the technical language of philosophy, existence is a 'secondary intelligible' (*maʿqūl thānī*), a generic term that applies to a number of objects but to which nothing concrete corresponds in the extra-mental world. It is like the copula, the 'is' in our sentences, which states that something does actually exist in the external world but says nothing about its 'whatness', i.e., its specific qualities, nature or identity. As all things partake of existence in a general way, what determines something as it is and distinguishes it from other actually existing beings is its essence or 'quiddity' (*māhiyya*). In this sense, essence takes precedence over existence and leads to the doctrine of the primacy of essence over existence (*aṣālat al-māhiyya*). As we shall see later, Suhrawardī's mistake was to equate the concept and reality of existence and treat existence, the very principle by which all things come to exist, as a mental abstraction.

After following Suhrawardī through his own teacher Mīr Dāmād, Ṣadrā left the doctrine of the primacy of essence, arguing that metaphysical essentialism gives us not the reality itself but a mental picture of it. Essence is what emerges in the mind as a representation of actually existing beings and can never be a substitute for their actual reality in the extra-mental world. Both reason and intuition suggest that there is more to reality than our mental representations of it and that the human mind, no matter how competent it is, cannot encapsulate the reality of things even at the level of pure representation. Furthermore, revelation, the third source of knowledge, presents a metaphysics of creation that cannot be fully explained with an essentialist ontology and temporal cosmology. Ṣadrā needed a new ontology to explain the utter contingency of the world vis-à-vis God's absolute reality as the Transcendent principle and source of all things. As we shall discuss later, he also needed a radically new epistemology to ground all cognition and knowledge-related terms in existence.

CRISIS IN METHODOLOGY

The second crisis of philosophical thinking in Islam was methodological in nature with grave consequences for the way we know the universe. The extreme confidence of the Peripatetic philosophers in unaided reason not only mistreated some central issues in religious metaphysics but also neglected the existential foundations of virtues and the role of spiritual knowledge in philosophical analysis. Ṣadrā does not in any way impute impiety to the philosophers, let alone infidelity, and disagrees with Ghazālī's harsh attacks on the Peripatetics. Instead, he stresses the delicate balance between revelation, human reason and intuition. But he does criticize the philosophers for not taking their philosophical premises to their logical conclusion and for failing to establish spiritual realization as the ultimate goal of philosophical reflection. He sees no contradiction between logico-philosophical analysis and intuitive, spiritual knowledge. A proper philosophical outlook based on the centrality of existence makes thinking an exercise in existence and its various modalities. It also leads to knowledge as spiritual 'witnessing' and 'presence'. Without recovering this meaning of thinking, Ṣadrā argues, there is no future for philosophy.

Ṣadrā's attempt to dovetail philosophical thinking with spiritual wayfaring was not simply a matter of personal taste. It was grounded in the ontological vision that he developed to explain the way things are. Since existence is the ground of all metaphysics, what we call reality is ultimately a particular manifestation of existence and cannot stand on its own. It is grounded in a principle higher than the total sum of empirical evidence, logical deduction and rational argumentation. If reality is one and cannot be reduced to one of its components, the methods by which we study it must also reflect this unity. It is the philosopher's task to study each aspect of reality according to its own specific state and nature. Just as there are 'degrees of existence' (*marātib al-wujūd*), there are also degrees of knowledge corresponding to them. In tandem with Ṣadrā's conceptual realism, there is no veritable knowledge without a corresponding reality that grounds it in existence. The goal of knowledge is to reach that reality, not construct a mental picture of it. The seeker of knowledge must, then, know that the 'method' in the broad sense of the term is only a tool to understand reality, not a substitute for it.

Had the previous schools of thought succeeded in developing a multilayered methodology? Ṣadrā does not think so. This crisis in methodology is a result of shortcomings in the ontological framework within which we formulate our methodological presuppositions. More importantly, the fact that something, in fact anything, can be studied from multiple perspectives is not a statement about our subjective approaches or points of view but about the way things are. Reality is such that it lends itself to multiple perspectives or what Sadara calls 'considering' (*iʿtibār*). Since all beings possess multiple layers of reality, it only makes sense to 'consider' them from several standpoints. Ṣadrā assigns such importance to this that he even quotes a saying to the effect that without the principle of 'multiple considerations' (*al-iʿtibārāt*), 'wisdom would have been lost' (*Īqāẓ*, 54). This grounding of 'perspectivalism' in ontology helps Ṣadrā deal with seemingly contradictory issues and positions in philosophy. It also opens up new possibilities for the study of the history of philosophy from multiple points of view.

Ṣadrā's writings show that he was extremely knowledgeable about the history of Greek and Islamic philosophy, and of the various schools of thought in the Islamic period. His major works are replete with references to previous thinkers and their approaches to a particular problem. Pythagoreans, Platonists, Aristotelians, pre-Islamic Iranian philosophers, Muslim Peripatetics, Ashʿaris, Muʿtazilis, the Illuminationists, Ibn ʿArabī and his followers, and others, are discussed in Ṣadrā's works from multiple points of view. The plurality of schools of thought and their distinct and often contradictory methods must have been a source of concern for Ṣadrā as a student and teacher of philosophy. How do you teach your students when you are confronted with so many different perspectives? How do you work through the intricacies of subtle philosophical and theological problems without losing the integrity of your own thought?

These are valid methodological questions for any teacher of philosophy. But Ṣadrā's concern was not to try out different methodologies and decide on a medial point. Rather, his primary goal was to understand reality as a dynamic, multi-layered and continuous manifestation of existence, and make our epistemic perspectives and methodological tools conform to this reality. Empirical knowledge, observation, verification, logical demonstration, rational analysis, intuitive knowledge, direct witnessing, spiritual realization, mystical experience, and so on, are not simply different types of knowledge; they correspond to different levels of reality with specific qualities and attributes.

TWO PATHS OF KNOWING

Among the different types of knowing, Ṣadrā pays particular attention to two and calls them the path of *baḥth*, i.e., 'rational investigation' and *dhawq*, i.e., 'direct tasting'. The first path is the philosophers' way of studying reality with unaided reason. The second pertains in a general way to the mystics and denotes a state of knowing rather than a method in the conventional sense of the term. The philosophers hold that reality is structured in a rational way and thus lends itself to empirical investigation and logical analysis. The rational method does not impose the mind's contents on the universe but uncovers the rational order built into the nature of things. This is how al-Fārābī, Ibn Sīnā and Ibn

Rushd understood the rational method and considered it to be in perfect harmony with the Qurʾānic way of inference. On several occasions, Ṣadrā says that he has written the *Asfār* according to the 'speculative, demonstrative method' and his magnum opus in systematic philosophy is addressed to the people of 'rational investigation' (*al-Mabdaʾ*, i. 5). In his other works, he employs 'a different divine method and a new sacred style' (*Īqāẓ*, 7).

Is reality reducible to what can be captured by rational analysis alone? Ṣadrā holds that the rational method is a perfectly good and veritable way of studying certain aspects of reality but cannot claim to encapsulate all of it. Empirical-logical analysis works for certain degrees of existence and unveils their rational, orderly structure. The regularity that we see in nature is an extension of the built-in intelligibility of things and they are what Einstein has called 'reason incarnate'. While the laws of nature account for the order and structure of things as they are, they also lend themselves to empirical, scientific analysis. But there are levels of reality that do not lend themselves to purely empirical or rational investigation and require different ways of knowing. This is where Ṣadrā turns to the second method mentioned above, i.e., the path of 'tasting'.

In contrast to logical inference and rational analysis, 'tasting' as a way of knowing is based not on mental abstraction but on a direct, unmediated experience of reality. Rational proofs are second-order conceptualizations constructed through conceptual abstraction. By contrast, 'tasting' and 'witnessing' (*mushāhada*) are ways of direct seeing which unveils aspects of existence that are not available to empirical observation or rational abstraction. Unveiling, witnessing, presence, illumination and clearing as modes of knowing refer to different modalities of existence. The type of intuitive and mystical knowledge which Ṣadrā takes to be complementing rational knowledge is related to both divine mysteries and the multiple modes of existence. From the point of view of the subject who has the experience of witnessing and unveiling, the difference between knowledge based on abstraction and direct witnessing is comparable to the difference between knowing something and living it. Ṣadrā says that 'the difference between the sciences based on theory and the sciences based on vision is like the difference between someone who knows the definition of sweetness and someone who has actually tasted sweetness; and someone who understands the definition of health and power and someone who is actually healthy and powerful' (*Tafsīr*, vii. 10).

This type of knowledge gives us not just a concept but an experience of the reality before which we 'stand' in the full sense of the term and which can be attained through spiritual discipline and journeying. It also requires a different kind of language to express the 'ecstasy of existence', i.e., the gushing forth of the infinite possibilities of the all-inclusive reality of existence as 'penetrating existence' and the 'Breath of the Compassionate'. Ṣadrā states that 'the sciences of tasted knowledge and spiritual states cannot be fitted into the clothes of letters and words as they deserve to be stated. Whoever has not tasted has not known' (*Īqāẓ*, 8). The principle of the ineffable also applies to 'God's word' which in this context we might interpret as God's creative act: 'The secret of God's word is more sublime than to be contained by human language' (*Tafsīr*, vi. 6).

For Ṣadrā, the kind of knowledge obtained through witnessing, seeing, clearing and presence is not contradicted or overruled by rational-demonstrative knowledge. In fact, one of the signal achievements of Ṣadrā's Transcendent Wisdom is the complementarity between the two types of knowledge, which are also two methods and two states of knowing. Ṣadrā believes that one can have a spiritual vision and articulate it as a philosophical truth without jeopardizing either the realness of the experience or the cogency of the argument. Referring to the metaphysician Sufis before him, he says that 'we have indeed made their unveiling, based on tasting, correspond to the principles of demonstration' (*Asfār*, iii. 1. 263). Of course, this is still a matter of transposing a first-order experience into a second-order conceptualization and what happens in the process has far-reaching implications for conceptual realism. Ṣadrā's main concern, however, is to demonstrate that these two types of knowing are grounded in the multilayered architecture of existence.

DIVINE KNOWLEDGE

As for the Qurʾān as a source of knowledge, Ṣadrā embraces it wholeheartedly as any pious philosopher would do, and describes it as 'a nourishment for pure hearts and a remedy for sick souls' (*Tafsīr*, vi. 11). The Qurʾān is not an index or encyclopedia; one does not consult it like an ordinary book even though jurists, linguists, exegetes, theologians and others do refer to it for their specific issues. It is a 'book of guidance' for humanity (*al-Baqara*, 2: 2) and covers the most fundamental issues relating to the human state, the universe and God. It provides an outlook, a *Weltanschauung*, through which we are made to understand the reality of things as a whole, relate them to a higher principle which comprises them, and learn how to act morally according to the nature of things. Qurʾānic rationality has its own logic and does not contradict philosophical argumentation. As a matter of fact, 'religious law (*al-sharʿ*) combined with reason is light upon light' (*Uṣūl*, 438). Reason guided by revelation opens itself up to a principle higher than itself and thus gains a wider view of things. Revelation articulated by reason becomes capable of unveiling its multiple degrees of truth and meaning. Ṣadrā considers both as essential for attaining the truth and warns against 'pretentious philosophers who are deprived of the prophetic legacy and Muḥammadan Sharīʿa' (*al-Mabdaʾ*, i. 11).

As author of an unfinished commentary on the Qurʾān, Ṣadrā integrates Qurʾānic verses, stories, metaphors and themes into his philosophical, cosmological and psychological works. For him, the Qurʾān is the ultimate source of 'essential knowledge' that contains the fundamental truths needed for man's perfection and proximity to the Divine: 'Whatever there is [to know] from the knowledge of the Lord, issues related to the Divine, demonstrative philosophy and knowledge based on unveiling is to be found in the Qurʾān with their principle, branch, beginning, goal, fruit and essence – so much so that each chapter in the Qurʾān contains the ultimate goal of the ideas of the previous philosophers and the end of the secrets of the ancient saints' (*Tafsīr*, vi. 5).

PHILOSOPHY AND THE SEARCH FOR THE TRANSCENDENT

Seeking to know God in the widest sense of the term lies at the heart of the Transcendent Wisdom. The 'four intellectual journeys', which we discussed in Chapter 1, cover the great chain of being and prepare the seeker of knowledge for the ultimate encounter with the Truth. The goal of scientific investigation, philosophical reflection and spiritual refinement is to attain a moral and intellectual state in which we can know God as the truth and source of all that exists. In Ṣadrā's words, 'the highest of the arts and the noblest of the deeds of the heart and the actions of one's capacity is the attainment of the art which some call wisdom and philosophy, and it is to be like the True God (*al-tashabbuh bi-l-ilāh al-ḥaqq*) and coming closer to Him to the extent possible for humans' (*Tafsīr*, vi. 3). The fulfillment of the human state is also related to realizing the Divine truth: 'Attaining the truth of divine unity is among the highest states of humanity' (*Īqāẓ*, 4).

Philosophy as the art of becoming 'God-like' takes us on a journey from our minds and physical phenomena to God and back, enabling us to travel through the great chain of being and rediscover the fundamental meaning of things. This circular path of philosophy is based on the multilayered and integrated nature of reality, which we can know to the extent possible only by investigating it from multiple perspectives. This is where ontology, epistemology, cosmology, theology, psychology and other branches of traditional philosophy come together to produce a holistic picture of reality. The ultimate goal of philosophy, however, is neither mental gymnastics nor conceptual cleverness. Rather, it is to understand the reality of things so that we can act accordingly, i.e., imitate God, come close to Him and lead a virtuous life. This is confirmed by Ṣadrā's definition of philosophy: 'Philosophy is the perfection of the human soul through the knowledge of the truths of existing beings as they are, and to establish their existence with demonstrative arguments, not through conjecture and imitation, to the extent possible for the human state' (*Asfār*, i. 1. 20).

Does the definition of philosophy reduce philosophy to theology and/or ethics? The task Ṣadrā assigns to philosophy goes beyond both theology and ethics in the conventional senses of those terms. No theological problem can be addressed properly, Ṣadrā holds, without first establishing its philosophical principle. Many of the theological conundrums which the theologians have created for themselves are a result of misconceiving the problem in the first place and failing to understand how existence as the principle of the transcendent behaves in the world of creation. Philosophy as love of wisdom is also different from the Peripatetics' practice in that the fundamental truths of philosophy cannot be attained through speculative thinking alone; the seeker of knowledge must be existentially involved in the truth of what he seeks to attain. Finally, philosophical reflection is also different from what Ṣadrā calls pretentious 'Sufi imaginings', i.e., ascetic practice and imaginary speculation without intellectual content. Philosophy as wisdom is based on a sustained commitment to philosophical enquiry, sound proof and spiritual discipline all at once:

This wisdom does not issue from theological disputations, nor from popular imitations, nor from blameworthy investigative philosophy, nor from Sufi imaginings. Rather, it is a result of learning lessons from contemplation of the message of the verses of God and meditation upon the dominion of His heavens and His earth with a strong aversion to that to which the nature of the people of disputation and the majority are drawn and a complete rejection of what the hearts of ordinary people have accepted as beautiful. (*Mashāʿir*, §2.)

PHILOSOPHY AND THEOLOGY

Having established the knowledge of God and virtuous life as among the primary goals of philosophy, Ṣadrā raises the following question: How do we know God without undermining His absolute truth and unity on the one hand, and without jeopardizing the integrity of philosophical investigation on the other? This poses a serious challenge to both the theologian and the philosopher. For the theologian, the problem is the relevance of philosophical arguments to prove the existence of God and to explain the universe as a system which needs a transcendent principle, i.e., a creator by which it is created and sustained. Furthermore, if the sacred scripture contains all the truth, why do we need rational, linguistic and scholastic arguments to prove God's existence or His dominion over the universe?

For the philosopher, the challenge is to show that introducing a transcendent principle such as God into philosophical enquiry does not undercut philosophy or trump the demands of reason. The issue is further complicated by the qualitative differences between the Aristotelian notion of the Divine as the Unmoved Mover and the theistic concept of God as the Creator, Master, Sustainer and Destroyer of all things. To what extent the Peripatetic philosophers have succeeded in this task is still an open question. Yet it has led to a long and checkered controversy in Islamic intellectual history. Ghazālī's verdict has been the harshest on the philosophers claiming that the Aristotelian metaphysics which the Muslim philosophers adopted without much critical reflection is incapable of explaining how God creates and sustains the universe. Ghazālī's overall conclusion was that the Peripatetic philosophers had left us with two choices: either choose pious metaphysics and jettison systematic philosophy or embrace Aristotelian metaphysics and give up the God of the Abrahamic tradition.

Ṣadrā addresses these challenges by expanding the meaning of philosophy to include a close study of the concept and reality of existence. His main quarrels with the theologians are not so much about specific arguments but about the way in which the theological-juridical tradition tends to impoverish serious philosophical thinking in the name of safeguarding God and religion against the arrogant tendencies of discursive reason. His advice to the philosophers is to realize that no philosophical enquiry can deliver without grasping the central reality of existence which, by definition, goes beyond the individual mind.

Ṣadrā does not see himself bound by either theology or philosophy. Instead, he subscribes to the path of the '*rabbāniy-yūn*', those who follow the 'ways of the Lord'. The following selections from the *Mashāʿir* state that there are many paths to God but there is also a hierarchy of the methods by which the best philosophical discourse can be developed about God. The way to God and back is, again, through the proper study of existence:

Know that the paths to God, transcendent is He, are multiple, because He possesses countless virtues and aspects, 'and each one has a goal to which he turns' (*al-Baqara*, 2: 143).[1] However, certain of them are more luminous and of superior virtue and more rigorous and possess firmer demonstrations. The most trust-worthy path and the one of the greatest virtues leading to Him, His Qualities and His Actions is the one in which the middle term in the demonstration is none other than He. In this case, the path leading to the desired object comes from the desired object itself because He is the proof of all things. And this was the path of all the prophets and the people of sincerity, may the peace of God be upon them all. 'Say – This is my way: I call on God with clear vision, I and whosoever follows me' (*Yūsuf*, 12: 108). 'This is in the earliest books of revelation, the book of Abraham and Moses' (*Aʿlā*, 87: 17). And these are those who seek the witness of God – transcendent is He – through Himself. 'God himself is witness that

1 Ṣadrā complements this with a poem: 'The names describing You are many but Your goodness is one/And everything refers to this beauty.' (*Īqāẓ*, 22)

there is no God save He' (*Āl ʿImrān*, 3: 16). Then they seek to bear witness through the Divine Essence to His Divine Attributes, and one after another through His Attributes to His Acts and Effects. (*Mashāʿir*, 142)

This is a soft criticism of natural theology, which takes the world as its starting point and moves to its Designer or Creator. Theologians and philosophers have made use of natural theology to explain the orderly structure of the universe and to show why it is logical to move from the rationality built into the universe to a supreme mind, i.e., God.

Others take recourse to the knowledge of His Essence – transcendent is He – and of His Attributes by the intermediary of something other than He. Thus the majority of the philosophers take recourse to contingency, the philosophers of nature to the movement of the body [of the universe], the theologians to the creation of the world in time, etc. And these [foregoing proofs] are also reasons and witnesses. However, this path [of which we have spoken] is the most firm and of the greatest virtue. In fact, it is to these different paths that the Divine Book alludes when He – transcendent is He – says, 'We shall show them our signs on the horizons and within their souls until it will become manifest unto them that it is the truth' (*Fuṣṣilat*, 41: 53). And it is to this path that allusion is made in His word, 'does not thy Lord suffice since He is witness over all things?' (*Fuṣṣilat*, 41: 53). (*Mashāʿir*, 143)

This is a more specific version of natural theology and focuses on the intrinsic qualities of the physical universe. Ṣadrā relates contingency, motion and other properties of the corporeal world to God's Names and Qualities as they, in their multiplicity, generate the various modalities of existence. But the most trusted method, the one that is both rational and salvific, is the one which takes God Himself as its starting point.

The sages of the Lord (*rabbāniyyūn*) first of all look at the reality of *wujūd*. Then they realize it and come to know that it is the principle of all things and that it is, according to the truth, the Necessary Being. As for contingency, indigence, and the state of being caused, these are conditions adjoined to *wujūd* not because of the reality of *wujūd* but because of the deficiencies and non-existence, which are extrinsic to the source of its reality. Then by looking at what requires necessity and contingency, richness and indigence, they reach the unity of His Attributes and through the understanding of His Attributes to the how-ness of His States and Effects. (*Mashāʿir*, §144)

This is called the 'proof of the veracious' (*burhān al-ṣiddiqīn*), which Ṣadrā takes to be superior to all other proofs for the existence of God. Instead of moving from effect to cause or from motion to the mover, this proof considers existence as the beginning and end of all things. Since no being more perfect than God can be conceived, He must exist in the most perfect and fullest sense of the term. Ṣadrā thus takes God Himself as the proof of Himself and everything else. While natural theology tries to prove the existence of what is infinite and absolute by inferring from the properties of what is finite and limited, the 'proof of the veracious' bypasses all accidental and relative existence and instead concentrates on God as the Absolute and Necessary Existence.

EXISTENCE AND GOD

How does existence relate to God? Ṣadrā's elaborate deliberations on existence suggest that existence is the face of God turned towards the world of creation. Existence is neither a mental concept nor a 'thing' among other things. Rather, it is the principle by which things exist. It is by participating in the reality of existence that beings obtain meaning, intelligibility, order and structure. 'Existing' is a mode of participation; it is to partake of the all-inclusive and penetrating reality of existence. When we say that the tree in the garden exists, we refer not to a substance standing on its own but to a particular mode of existence which delimits itself into what we call 'tree'. The particularization (*takhaṣṣuṣ*) of existence into specific individual beings is a key component of the ontology of the world of multiplicity and reinforces the dynamic relationship between oneness and multiplicity. For a philosopher like Ṣadrā, the dazzling plurality of substances and forms is only a manifestation of the underlying unity of existence and confirms its infinite possibilities.

Existence ties all beings to their source of existentiation, i.e., God. The various modalities and qualities of existence are not just ordinary existential properties by which we describe the physical qualities of things. Rather, they are, in the suggestive phrase of Rudolf Otto, 'saving actualities' which connect us to the Divine.[1] Inquiry into existence leads to a 'doctrine of salvation' because existence is now studied as a Divine theophany (*tajallī*), and the modalities of existence are seen as a manifestation of the Names and Qualities of God. Existence as the 'breath of the Compassionate' (*nafas al-raḥmān*) serves as a link between the Creator and the created, the Absolute and the relative, the Eternal and the transient. By failing to articulate the precise relationship between God and existence, the philosopher reduces metaphysics to the study of fixed substances and the theologian ends up with fideism. Both positions land us in a crisis of philosophy and theology. Ṣadrā's answer is to go back to the study of existence – a task which the theologians have never undertaken in a serious

1 Otto, *Mysticism East and West* (1960), 34.

manner and which the philosophers have undermined by equating existence with Aristotle's fixed substances.

Here we are faced with another conundrum in ontology and metaphysics. Since existence is never just the sum of particular existents, how do we know it? Can we know the reality of existence in separation from its particular members? It is equally valid to ask if it is possible to know individual existents apart from the larger reality of existence. In philosophy, this is known as the problem of 'aporetic ontology' where we perceive individual existents as 'individuals' on the one hand and as 'instances of a whole' on the other. When we study individual beings such as a tree or a horse, we consider them to be both particular beings in their own right and members of a larger class such as plants, animals, etc. Since there is no way to exhaust all empirical possibilities and enumerate all the possible members of a class, we operate with a general notion of a class or a whole. The same applies to the relationship between existents and existence: while I perceive particular existents, I also perceive them as part of a larger whole to which they belong.

This seemingly technical issue is crucial for Ṣadrā's ontology because it underlies his key claim that existence is always more than the sum total of particular existents. No classification, no matter how comprehensive it is, can encapsulate all the possibilities of existence. Existence defies easy categorizations. Ṣadrā further argues that the world is intrinsically and a posteriori saddled with structures of meaning, order, proportion and relations. It is not the case that there are 'bare facts' out there devoid of qualitative attributes to which the mind a posteriori assigns 'meaning'. Neither the fact–meaning distinction nor the fact–value distinction arises in Ṣadrean ontology because the ontological and axiological context of such terms as fact, object, meaning, value and so on is determined by the all-inclusive reality of existence.[1] Beings possess order, structure, proportion and meaning in an intrinsic and constitutive manner. As recent scientific studies in quantum mechanics have shown, this is an integral part of the way things are, and it explains how and why we perceive the world around us as whole, structured, ordered and interrelated.

KNOWING THE UNKNOWABLE GOD

At this point, a theologically relevant question arises: Where do we start to know God? With Himself or with the world of creation? Starting with God appears to be tautological because it involves the very term we want to prove in logical inference. Starting with the world means that we move from the particular instances of existence to the principle of existence or, in the language of theology, from the created to the Creator. The second method corresponds to natural theology. Ṣadrā accepts both methods in their own right but states that natural theology is a type of 'demonstrative argument' whereas the first method is the path of those who possess an intimate knowledge of God.

> Whoever has known the Truth [God] through the creation and with rational arguments has not really known the Truth in the way It should be known. Whoever has turned away from the creation and known the Truth with the Truth has truly known the Truth. With the former, you ascend and with the latter you descend [in hierarchy of existence]. The first is the path of those who contemplate the creation of the heavens and the earth 'so that it will become clear to them that He is the Truth' (*Fuṣṣilat*, 41: 53).

1 For more on this, see Ibrahim Kalin, *Knowledge in Later Islamic Philosophy* (2010), 237–8.

The second is the path of those veracious people who witness [the creation of the heavens and the earth] with the Truth, not by itself. It is referred to in His Sublime words: 'Is your Lord not sufficient [for proof] that He is a witness to all things' (*Fuṣṣilat*, 41: 53). They are the ones who are in a state of total attraction and love with the Truth, to whom a reference has been made in the hadith about becoming closer to God through supererogatory prayers (*nawāfil*)'.[1] (*Īqāẓ*, 47).

Ṣadrā clearly favours the second path of knowing God, i.e., 'proof of the veracious', but warns that it is not open to all. It requires a deep reflection on available rational proofs but with an eye to overcoming that so that we are not stuck in argumentative bickering. We can attain knowledge of God through Gestalt perception whereby senses, reason and intuition are united. Following the *via negativa*, Ṣadrā describes God as beyond all description including being and non-being. A true knower can get only a glimpse of this reality 'through a special path, and it is knowing the Truth (God) with the Truth (God) when the wayfarer becomes extinct and perishing in Him' (*Īqāẓ*, 22). Ultimately, though, no proof can be adduced for God's existence because He is the source of all proofs and the 'proof of everything':

... the Necessary Being has no proof, no definition and therefore no reason from a number of different points of view. It has no reason for existence like an active [agent] and ultimate goal, no

1 This is a reference to the famous hadith, reported in the *Ṣaḥīḥ* of Bukhārī and by others, that: 'My servant does not draw near to Me with anything more loved by Me than the religious duties I have imposed upon him, and My servant continues to draw near to Me with supererogatory works so that I shall love him. When I love him I am his hearing with which he hears, his seeing with which he sees, his hand with which he holds, and his foot with which he walks. Were he to ask [something] of Me, I would surely give it to him; and were he to ask Me for refuge, I would surely grant him it.'

reason for constitution (*al-qiwām*) like matter and form and no reason for quiddity like genus and differentia. In spite of this, nothing is hidden from Him; He is the proof of everything and closest to everything as He the Exalted said: 'And We are closer to you than your jugular vein' (*Qāf*, 50: 16). And He said: 'And He is with you wherever you are' (*Ḥadīd*, 57: 4). And He is the proof of His own Essence as He said: 'God testifies that there is no god but He'. He also said: 'Is your Lord not sufficient [as a proof] that He is a witness to all things' (*Fuṣṣilat*, 41: 53) and 'Say: What is greater as witness? Say: God.' (*Asfār*, i. 3. 399–400)

Knowing God, to the extent this is possible for the finite human mind, involves contemplating God as the ultimate beginning and end of all things. It also entails the study of God Himself and His actions: 'Without doubt, the noblest divine knowledge is the knowledge of the First Truth, His degree and His existence with His qualities of perfection and attributes of beauty, how His actions emanate, how existing beings begin with Him and how they return to Him' (*al-Mabda*ʾ, i. 5). In the language of philosophy, this is the great chain of being, the embedded network of the universe – the map of existence as it displays its infinite possibilities. Given the ontological qualities of the universe and our cognitive access to them, it is only by taking the world of existence as a whole that we can understand its parts.

THE PARADOX OF CREATION

But here we are faced with another philosophical-cum-theological problem and it is the paradox of creation: while creation is a testimony to God's existence and supreme art, it is also a veil that hides Him. The world is the best proof for the existence of God for a number of reasons. The order and harmony we see in the universe calls for an intelligent designer. The beauty we witness in the natural world points to a higher principle, a principle that is also the source of beauty, grace and compassion. God is not a distant clock-maker; the relationship between Him and His creation is neither mechanical nor mathematical. While remaining absolutely one and transcendent, He is involved in creation in the sense that He not only creates but also sustains and nourishes His creation. Just as causality requires a proper relationship between cause and effect, the existence of the universe necessitates the existence of God but not vice versa. This establishes an intimate relationship between God and creation. Ṣadrā states this point in clearly ontological terms: 'There is a secret here and it is the fact that the effect is nothing but a mode of the [self-]delimitation and transformation of the cause. Whoever has known the cause has also known its affairs and states' (*Īqāẓ*, 47).

While these descriptions give us an idea about the Creator, the world of creation is also deceptive in the sense that it veils God's absolutely clear and omnipresent existence. From both an ontological and moral point of view, the world acts as a veil, offering itself as a reality on its own, allowing us to forget the Reality behind all apperances. Concentrating on the world itself to the exclusion of the larger reality of which it is a part is a grave philosophical mistake and theological error. For a sage like Ṣadrā, it is futile to try to prove God's existence through the veil that hides Him. He is so evident that only those whose minds have been clouded and whose hearts have been tainted search for proofs for His existence. In Ṣadrā's strongly ontological language, the world in and of itself cannot be said to exist; otherwise, this would lead to two independently existing beings or realities, i.e., God and the world. All created beings must be totally dependent upon

God. In this sense, the world hides and veils God. Ṣadrā says that 'the contingent beings, whether subtle spiritual or opaque physical, are veils for His Essence, the Exalted...' (*Īqāẓ*, 46–7).

The way out of this conundrum is to see the world with 'two eyes', to use Ibn ʿArabī's suggestive phrase. On the one hand, God is absolutely transcendent, utterly different, and beyond any comparison. On the other hand, He is immanent, close and 'all-encompassing' (*al-muḥīṭ*). One can have a proper understanding of the Divine only by combining the two elements, i.e., *tanzīh*, transcendence, and *tashbīh*, immanence. Seeing God through the eye of transcendence alone leads to a mechanical deity cut off from the world. One cannot relate to such a God, cannot pray to Him, and so on. Considering God in His aspect of immanence alone runs the risk of relegating God to the level of His creation. This leads to pantheism, one of the worst errors in metaphysics because it fails to acknowledge God's absolute independence and power. The true sage sees the Divine through the two eyes of transcendence and immanence and knows that doing so leads not to two visions but to one.

Applying this principle to the way God and the world are related, Ṣadrā says: 'the true sage sees two mirrors: the mirror of the external world and the mirror of God and all the forms in them together without separating them' (*Īqāẓ*, 50). The true philosopher knows the difference between the world as a veil for God and as a proof for His existence. But it requires the combination of the two eyes of absoluteness and contingency: with one eye, he sees the world in itself, with the other in relation to the absolute. This is not just a subjective and psychological state. Rather, it is necessitated by the order of existence because all beings have two aspects, one referring to themselves and the other to God. Taken in and of itself, the world becomes an illusion, a veil that clouds our vision. Taken in relation to its source, the world becomes a 'sign', a proof, an artwork of God's creative act. This implies that we know the world of creation and the things in it not just by investigating their individual properties but also by recognizing the higher principle which governs them. This epistemological conclusion, too, is a necessity of the order of existence in which we are.

This leads us to what we may call the 'metaphysical transparency of the world'. The world is a limited reflection of God's infinite reality. Beings reflect God's dazzling light in proportion to their capacity to reflect light and to the extent to which they are transparent and luminous. 'All essences and contingent beings' says Ṣadrā, 'are mirrors for the existence of the Truth the Exalted and an abode (of reflection) for Its sacred reality.' The intrinsic value and intelligibility of the world of existence comes from its ability to witness God's absolute and infinite reality. But each being mirrors God in a different way. The more 'being-full' a thing is, the closer it is to reflecting the reality of existence. From the pure intelligibles to the sensibles, the entire cosmos serves as a mirror for God's beauty and generosity. Thus Ṣadrā says that 'sensible objects, because of the intensity of their veils, cannot properly disclose the Truth' (*Īqāẓ*, 61). Sensate beings are transient, decaying and unstable and thus cannot reflect what is permanent and transcendent. By contrast, spiritual and intelligible beings are ontologically closer to the source of existence and thus are better suited to mirror the reality of God. That's why the philosopher's primary object of concentration should be not senses or sensate objects but the *intelligibilia* (*maʿqūlāt*), which are immune from the death and destruction of the physical world. The paradox of creation can be overcome, then, by overcoming the contingency of the world and placing it within the larger context of existence as God's face turned to the world. A proper understanding of this point requires a proper study of the problem of existence.

EXISTENCE: THE CENTRAL QUESTION OF METAPHYSICS

Mullā Ṣadrā's most important contribution to philosophy is the study of existence as the foundational principle and reality of things. Ṣadrā's mature thought represents a paradigm shift from the Aristotelian metaphysics of fixed substances to the ontology of existence as the ultimate ground and source of reality. Ṣadrā holds that beings derive their reality and truth from their existence and that a proper philosophical analysis must therefore start with existence and eventually end with it. Existence is the central concept that links all realms of being and categories of cognition:

The problem of existence is the foundation of philosophical principles, the ground of metaphysical questions, and the pole around which rotates the millstone of the science of unity, the science of eschatology and the science of the resurrection of souls and bodies and many other things, which we have been the only person to demonstrate and the unique person to bring out [their meaning]. Whoever is ignorant of the knowledge of existence, his ignorance runs though the most important of all subjects and the greatest among them, and he will become heedless of it and the secrets of Divine knowledge and its inner meanings will become lost to him as well as the science of Divine Names and Qualities and prophecy and the science of the soul and its connections [with the whole of cosmology] and its return to the Origin of its origins and its final end [eschatology]. Therefore, we saw to it that we begin with it [the question of existence]. (*Mashāʿir*, §4)

Existence is the principal reality by which things exist. It is not a 'concept' in the sense of an abstract term, though it has a conceptual mode of existence which we call 'mental existence'. It is not a 'thing' among other things though it is 'all things' at a certain level of existentiation. It is not a substance, accident or quality though it is all of them because, in the final analysis, there is nothing in reality except existence. It has no counterpart or opposite because neither 'essence' nor 'non-existence' (*ʿadam*) can claim to have the same degree of reality as existence. As Ṣadrā puts it,

> The reality of existence-qua-existence is not limited by generality and delimitation, universality and particularity, and inclusiveness and specificity. It is neither one [numerically] by a oneness added to it, nor many.... In its essence, it is nothing but full realization, actuality and manifestation. These meanings of contingency, concepts of universality, attributes of rational consideration, and terms of mental analysis are attached to it on account of its degrees and stations. (*Asfār*, i. 1. 259)

Existence self-determines itself into various modes and modalities and thus can be given many names and descriptions. Since it precedes and generates everything, it is wrong to say that such and such an object exists with certain properties. From an ontological point of view, it is more appropriate to say that existence unveils and delimits itself as a tree, as a mountain, as a relation, etc. Instead of saying that 'a black object exists', Ṣadrā would have us say that 'existence-as-black' has such-and-such qualities. Existence qualified as such is

> by itself an existence and is renewed continuously and divided into antecedent, subsequent, deficient and complete. It has parts and individuals some of which vanish, some emerge and some are yet to come... this single and continuous existence is also a conjoined and changing existence. This is also true for all of its parts. Thus it has oneness that expands to [its] numbers for it is

oneness that comprises [all of its parts]. Therefore if we say 'it is one', we would be right. If we say 'it is many', we would be right. If we say 'it is the same from the beginning of change to the end', we would be right. If we say 'it is changing at every moment', we would be right. If we say 'it is existent with all of its components', we would be right. And if we say 'it is non-existent', we would be right. (*Ḥudūth*, 70–1)

Since existence is neither a thing nor a concept but rather the principle of 'full realization, actuality and manifestation', the Peripatetic philosophers were wrong to assume that existence could be explained in terms of substances and their properties. Substances can only be a subcategory of existence. The essentialists, which include most of the Ashᶜaris and the Muᶜtazilis as well as the School of Illumination, were also mistaken in presuming that existence is a secondary intelligible, a general concept to which in reality nothing corresponds. This description applies to existence only as a mental object, not as a concrete reality, which defies conceptual abstraction. A logical definition of existence is not possible because it has no genus and differentia. It cannot be 'made known through description (*taᶜrīf*)' either, because description is done through something better known; but there is nothing more known and apparent than existence. It is our minds that fail to see the absolutely clear and distinct reality of existence. The reason for this 'fundamental failure' is that our minds can perceive only concepts and abstract notions whereas existence is always a concrete reality in the sense of having 'specific effects', realization, delimitation, etc. For Ṣadrā, one of the goals of philosophy is to equip us with the proper epistemic tools and cognitive means to 'see' the self-evident (*badīhī*) reality of existence. This, however, cannot be achieved by mental or rational analysis alone because demonstrative and rational analyses give us only a mental picture of existence, not its reality.

THE CONCEPT AND REALITY OF EXISTENCE

Ṣadrā never tires of reminding us that existence is a dynamic and multifaceted reality that defies abstraction and conceptualization. To underscore this point, he introduces a key distinction between the concept and reality of existence. The 'concept of existence' (*mafhūm al-wujūd*) is a mental representation of existence and reveals something of its conceptual structure. As the human mind works with concepts and general and abstract terms, it turns existence, like everything else, into a concept. It then applies this concept to a multitude of objects and classes. The 'reality of existence' (*ḥaqīqat al-wujūd*), however, remains beyond mental constructions and generalizations. The concept of existence is like a single-shot picture taken from a stream of water, frozen and enlarged for analysis and inspection. The moment we take that picture, we have already left the level of concrete, actual reality and entered the sphere of abstraction. As we look at that frame, we know that reality has already passed by us. The philosopher is expected to realize that concepts are our mental tools, useful and indispensable, but eventually removed from the reality which is ever flowing, dynamic and organic. In Ṣadrā's words:

> Every concrete being represented in the mind with its reality ought to maintain its quiddity despite the change in its modality of existence. The reality of existence is such that it is in the extra-mental world. Everything whose reality is such that it is in the extra-mental world cannot be found [as it is] in the mind, otherwise this would lead to the alteration of something from its own reality [into something else]. Therefore the reality of existence cannot be found in any mind. What is represented of existence in the soul

whereby it takes on universality and generality is not the reality of existence but one of the aspects of its constitution and one of its names. (*Asfār*, i. 1. 37–8)

Here we detect a certain tension in classical ontology. The human mind works through concepts, ideas and abstractions, and the mind is bound to represent the world to itself as a 'picture' and 'image'. But even this picture is not static and immutable; it is constantly drawn and redrawn through careful conceptual analysis and investigation. But in the final analysis, it is a picture and represents a certain epistemic distance from the actuality of things. By contrast, existence is dynamic, continuous, self-renewing, self-effusing. It is also all-embracing in that it can leave nothing outside. This is underlined by Ṣadrā's oft-repeated premise that existence is not a thing among things but the fundamental principle by which all things come to exist. To use Ṣadrā's ontological vocabulary, the 'really existing things' (*al-wujūdāt*) are not those things that have 'matter' but those which transcend matter through intensification in existence (cf. *Asfār*, iii. 1. 304). 'Matter' and other physical properties, which we tend to identify as real beings, are just one aspect of existence and its modalities. To exist means to have more than material, corporeal existence. It means to be the substratum of 'existential effects' such as matter, movement, growth, generation, corruption, and so on.

What we mean by actual [i.e., external] existence is that the concomitants of an [actual] essence follow from it. When blackness is found in the external world, its proper nature is to cause absence of sight. The proper effect of hotness is to cause hotness. But when they occur in the soul, these concomitants do not follow from them. We call the former actual [external] existence and the latter mental existence. (*Asfār*, i. 3. 312)

In another place, Ṣadrā states the same point, this time focusing on what it means to be in the 'external world' and in the 'mind':

> It is clear that what we mean by 'the external world' and 'in the mind' when we say 'this exists in the external world' and 'that exists in the mind' is not one of substratum, place or subject. Instead, the meaning of something existing in the external world is that it has an existence to which effects and states [of existence] occur. Its existing in the mind means the opposite. If existence had no reality except the actualization of a quiddity, then there would remain no difference between the external and the mind. (*Mashāʿir*, §22)

The reality of existence constitutes the order of 'existential effects' and is the proper subject matter of fundamental ontology. By contrast, the concept of existence turns all of these existential properties into general notions, concepts and abstractions. Failing to understand this distinction between the two orders of reality, as Ṣadrā thinks Suhrawardī had done (*Asfār*, iii. 1. 353), leads to all sorts of philosophical errors and fallacious conclusions about the multifaceted nature of existence.

THE ONE AND THE MANY

One of the recurring themes of Ṣadrā's thought is the formulation of different epistemologies corresponding to different levels of reality. While existence is one, it manifests itself through modes and modalities which generate the multiplicity of substances in the world of creation. In Ṣadrā's words: 'the modalities of existence have different degrees; some are intellective, some are related to the soul, and some are dark without any perception' (*Asfār*, iii. 1. 363). These levels and layers of manifestation are interconnected and hierarchical, moving from the One to the many and back to the One. There is only one single reality in existence but it travels through the entire 'circle of existence' (*dā'irat al-wujūd*) leaving a different mark at every level of manifestation and self-delimitation. Existence remains the single immutable reality at the root of all things. But it also displays an infinite number of shades, colours, modes and modalities. This is what Ibn ʿArabī has called 'unity-in-plurality' (*al-waḥda fī l-kathrā*). This leads Ṣadrā to formulate one of the key principles of his epistemology: 'It is in the nature of the intellect to unite what is multiple and it is in the nature of the senses to multiply what is one' (*Asfār*, iii. 1. 380).

Plurality of forms points to the unity of source:

... actually existing beings are many in the external world but the source of their existence and the owner of their realization is one and single. And it is the reality of expanding being itself, not something else. The source of their plurality is self-determination. What is thus plural is judged to be really existing beings. Yet the consideration of their existing is different from the consideration of their plurality. Their existing is real but plurality is a matter of [mental] consideration. (*Asfār*, i. 2. 321)

Without denying the use and necessity of mental analysis, Ṣadrā proposes another way of attaining the reality of existence. In strikingly vivid language, he calls it 'illuminative presence' (*ḥuḍūr ishrāqī*) and 'direct witnessing' (*shuhūd ʿaynī*):

The reality of existence is not in any way actualized in its essence in any of the minds, because existence is not a universal concept and the existence of every existent is this existent itself *in concreto*, and that which is *in concreto* cannot be a mental concept. What is represented of existence as a general mental concept is the existence which one calls related existence, which is proper to logical judgements. As for knowledge of the reality of existence, that cannot be other than illuminative presence and real witnessing. Consequently, no doubt remains concerning its identity. (*Mashāʿir*, §57)

While existence links together all beings, substances and accidents, it also relates everything to God, the ultimate source and origin of things because existence, as we mentioned, is God's face turned to the world. In order to clarify the connection between God and existence, Ṣadrā develops a carefully articulated ontology to avoid the mistake of equating 'existence' with God. Being infinite and absolute and having no partner and likeness to Him, God is the Absolute Being (*al-wujūd al-muṭlaq*) which transcends all things, attributes and qualities including existence itself. In contrast to pantheism and panantheism, two similar metaphysical errors, existence is not God. Onto-theology, the idea that God is somehow the 'largest of all beings', is self-contradictory and cannot apply to God because God is the source of existence, not a modality of it. Existence is not one of the Divine Names like the Merciful (*al-raḥmān*) or the Creator (*al-khāliq*) either. God manifests Himself in the world of creation through His Names and Qualities, which reveal something of God's inner nature. Existence, however, belongs to a different category. It is neither God *per se* nor one of His Qualities but it cannot be something completely separate from Him either, otherwise we introduce an ontological duality which contradicts the most fundamental premise of monotheism.

In our daily conversations, we use the copula, which stands for existence in language, for all beings that exist. We say, for instance, that the tree there *is* tall, the weather *is* cold today, etc. In such statements, the copula 'is' refers to an existential property. We use the same language in regards to God and say that God exists, God *is* merciful, etc. But in reality, this is misleading because it attributes an ontological property to God who is already the ultimate source of existence. God is beyond the categories of existence and non-existence and cannot be said to exist or not exist in the ordinary sense of the term: 'The world of the Necessary Essence is beyond existence and non-existence; rather, it encapsulates them both' (*Īqāẓ*, 21). In Plotinus' terms, God is the Beyond-Being to which no ordinary qualities apply. We cannot say that God exists in the same way that humans, the sky or trees exist. There is an ontological and substantial difference among beings that exist with varying degrees of existentiation. Ordinary language usually blurs these distinctions and assumes a general state of existing for all beings. But the act of existing comes in different degrees of intensification, existential effects, priority and posteriority.

THREE TYPES OF EXISTENCE

Ṣadrā uses an elaborate vocabulary to explain the different degrees of existence and how it generates beings with varying ontological states. In a discussion of this critical point, he introduces three types of existence and assigns each an ontological function. The first is the 'Absolute Being', which is not related to anything other than itself and applies to God alone. Different schools of philosophical mysticism have given it different names: 'The invisible essence, the essence of the invisible, the absolute invisible, and the absolutely one essence' (*Īqāẓ*, 11). These descriptions are meant to emphasize the element of transcendence and otherness in regard to God who is beyond any definition and depiction because no finite description can encompass that which is infinite.

The second type is 'related' or 'relative existence' which includes all created beings from intellects and souls to spheres and elements. Related existence refers to beings that have two ontological aspects: themselves and their source of existence. In regard to themselves, all beings are 'absolute' in the sense of being full, integral, self-standing entities. But this is so only by way of abstraction because all beings are derived from a source of existence and no entity can claim self-sufficiency in the grand scheme of things. In regard to themselves, beings are relative, imperfect, shadowy, dependent, and so on. It is only in regard to their source that they can be properly said to exist:

> The meaning of contingency in particular beings, which radiate from the True One, goes back to their deficiency and essential poverty and their being essentially related to [the Creator] whereby their origination is impossible without their self-sufficient maker. They have no essence in themselves except that they are related to the First Truth and dependent on It as God the Exalted said 'God is rich and you are poor' (*Muḥammad*, 47: 38). (*Ḥudūth*, 28–9)

The third type of existence is called 'the absolute expanding existence', which functions like a gateway between the first two. It underscores the ontological connection between self-sufficiency and contingency, between completeness and ontological poverty. To explain this point and relate it to God, Ṣadrā quotes ʿAlāʾ al-Dawla Simnānī's gloss on a passage in Ibn ʿArabī's *al-Futuḥāt al-Makkiyya*: 'The True Existence is God the Exalted, the Absolute Existence is His Act, and the delimited existence is His Effect. And what is meant by the general Absolute Existence is not the abstract concept [of existence] but expanding [existence]' (*Īqāẓ*, 15).

Ṣadrā then relates this philosophical discussion to the Qurʾānic verse (*al-Qaṣaṣ,* 28: 88) 'all things perish except His Face'. While offering his own commentary on the verse, Ṣadrā quotes from al-Ghazālī's *Mishkāt al-anwār*: 'everything, when considered from the point of view of its own essence, is nothing but pure non-existence. When it is considered from the point of view of the way in which existence moves into it from the First Truth, it is considered existing, not in its own essence but in relation to that which befits its source of existence. What truly exists (*al-mawjūd*) is thus God's face alone' (*Īqāẓ*, 29).

Here it is worth quoting Ṣadrā again to see how he develops the idea of absolutely unrelated, self-sufficient, necessary being in contrast to everything else:

According to the verifiers (*muḥaqqiqīn*) among the sages (*ʿurafāʾ*) and the theosophers (*mutaʾallihīn*) among the philosophers (*ḥukamāʾ*), it is clear and firmly established that the existence of everything is nothing but the reality of its identity, which is related to the existence of the Real and Self-Subsisting One and which is the basis of judgment for the being-ness of things. The most appropriate way to describe this is to say that [their existence] is a mode of their actual identity, which is related to the Divine Existence. We will establish further proofs for the fact that existential identities are among the degrees of the manifestation of His Essence and rays of His Majesty and Beauty. (*Asfār*, i. 1. 116)

The ontological premise that every particular being is a manifestation of the self-determination and particularization of the one single existence has radical implications for knowledge:

The perception of everything is therefore nothing but a consideration of this thing in a way that is related to the Necessary [Being] from this point of view, i.e., the fact that [the Necessary Being] is its existence and being-ness (*mawjūdiyya*). And this is not possible without perceiving the essence of the Real One the Exalted... Whoever perceives anything in any mode of perception perceives the Creator. People may be ignorant of this perception except for the elect from among the Friends of God the Exalted as it was reported from the Commander of the Believers [ʿAlī ibn Abī Ṭālib] who said: 'I have seen nothing but God before it, after it, with it, and in it.' All of these [perceptions] are correct. It is thus obvious that this simple perception of the Real One the Exalted obtains for every one of His servants. But this does not lead to the perception of God with all of His Essence because this is impossible as it was proved before.' (*Asfār*, i. 1. 117)

PRIMACY OF EXISTENCE

Ṣadrā establishes existence as the principal reality that precedes and constitutes all things. This is known as the 'primacy of existence' (*aṣālat al-wujūd*) and is usually contrasted with Suhrawardī's essentialist metaphysics based on the 'primacy of essence' (*aṣālat al-māhiyya*). Suhrawardī held that existence is a common term applicable to individual beings, a 'secondary intelligible' (*al-maʿqūl al-thānī*), a universal to be found only in the mind. What gives things their identity is their essence rather than existence because, Suhrawardī thought, to know that both man and horse *exist* adds nothing to our knowledge of them. Existence is thus nothing more than a common term between man and horse. What distinguishes them from one another is their quiddity, which defines the horse as an animal and man as a rational being. Even though Suhrawardī substitutes 'light' (*al-nūr*) for existence and develops what we might call a 'metaphysics of light', certain aspects of which Ṣadrā has incorporated into his thinking, the primacy of existence versus quiddity remains a fundamental point of difference between the two philosophers. In some respects, the long controversy between the 'essentialists' and 'existentialists' constitutes one of the most decisive moments in the history of Islamic thought.

Ṣadrā's own teacher Mīr Dāmād followed Suhrawardī and held that 'existence' functions like an auxiliary for actually existing substances. Reality is constituted by actually existing beings whose identities are established by essence or quiddity.

In Mīr Dāmād's words, existence is the 'story of a substance' in actual reality, nothing more. Here is how he formulates his position:

The existence of something in any substratum or state is the actualization of that thing in that substratum, not the attachment or appendage of something else to it. Otherwise what is simple [non-composite] would become composite. The establishment of something in [or by] itself is the establishment of that thing for itself. Whoever considers the existence of essence to be an attribute among the actual attributes or something among the mental beings beyond the concept of the originating existence, he is not one of the people worth having a discussion with, nor is he among the people of the truth, as it has been said by our previous partners in the art [of philosophy]. If the matter were to be as he assumed, then existence itself would become one of the essences, in which case its existence would become superadded to its essence just like the other contingent essences. Furthermore, its existence too would become its originating actualization, just like the existence of beings.

Therefore existence in the extra-mental world is the establishment of something in the extra-mental world, not that by which something becomes established in the extra-mental world. By the same token, existence in the mind is its occurrence in the mind. And the existence of every accident is its accident in its substratum. And the existence of existence is the existence of its substratum. A being that is caused [by a cause] and its essence is instaurated by the instaurator in a simple manner. Thus existence is the story of a substance instaurated in actual reality. (*Qabasāt*, 37)

In sharp contrast to the Ishraqi tradition and his own teacher, Ṣadrā holds that existence is the only reality that existentiates things, i.e., make them exist as concrete beings. Just as we do not say 'whiteness is white', we do not say that 'existence exists'. Whiteness is what makes things white, not a quality attributed to things that are already white. By the same token, things exist because they *are*, not because they *have* existence as an attribute. Claiming otherwise would be contradictory because it would suggest that things first exist independent of existence and then assume it as an attribute. In other words, it would lead to the illogical conclusion that things precede existence and thus exist before existence. To call something a 'thing', i.e., an actually existing being with real attributes and effects, is to confirm that it already exists. What makes this possible, however, is not the thing itself but existence because things exist only when they partake of existence. There is no way to circumscribe and encircle existence and declare that things exist independent of it. To paraphrase Wittgenstein's famous comment on the limits of language, we cannot step outside existence and establish things as independent entities in reality.

Ṣadrā goes a step further and argues that the distinction between essence and existence exists only in our minds. The mind, which is tuned to perceive things through abstract concepts and generalizations, analyses actually existing beings into two components called essence and existence. It asks two main questions: whether something *is* and *what* it is. The first question pertains to the existence or non-existence of something. The second relates to the essence of that thing, which distinguishes it from other beings. As Ṣadrā holds that it is existence that is the principal reality, he also maintains that essence is what the mind abstracts from an actual instantiation of existence. Essence is subsumed under existence but the mind works in a different way and takes essence to be prior to existence:

... essence is united with existence *in concreto* in a kind of essential unity. When the mind analyses them into two things, it asserts the precedence of one over the other *in concreto*. Now, this [the reality that precedes the other] is existence because it is the principle in being the reality emanating from the [First] Principle. As for the essence, it is united with and predicated of existence not like an attached accident but in its own reality [as essentially united with existence]. Insofar as the mind is concerned, the essence precedes the latter [i.e., existence] because essence is the principle in mental judgments. (*Asfār*, i. 1. 56)

GRADATION OF EXISTENCE

Existence establishes things as real existents but with varying degrees of intensity. While all things partake of existence in one way or another, they do not exist univocally because not all beings display the same level of complexity, vitality, intensity, intelligence, and so on. Logically and grammatically, we use the copula 'is' for all things that exist to affirm that they exist: the tree in my garden, stars, my pen 'are'. In other words, they exist as concrete beings with specific existential 'effects' and properties. But ontologically speaking, there is a substantial difference in the way beings exist. To account for this ontological complexity, Ṣadrā introduces the concept of *tashkīk al-wujūd* translated variously as the 'systematic ambiguity of existence', 'modulation of being', 'analogical gradation of existence' and 'amphiboly'.

In technical terms, gradation of existence states that existence is predicated of beings 'equivocally' (*ḥaml bi-l-tashkīk*), not 'univocally' (*ḥaml bi-l-tawāṭi'*). It holds that the degree of existence we find in individual beings increases or decreases in proportion to what sorts of ontological properties they possess. Things are ontologically 'stronger' or 'weaker' in virtue of their proximity to or distance from the source of existence. God as the Necessary Being and man as contingent being *exist* but with differing degrees of ontological intensity. This is comparable to different types of light: while the sun has the most intense light, the moon has only a reflection of it. Compared to them, the light of the candle is further diminished. This suggests that beings have higher and lower degrees of ontological properties, attributes and effects. To quote Ṣadrā:

As for its equivocal predication by primacy, priority, precedence and intensity, this is so because, as we shall explain, existence requires itself in some beings, has precedence in some in terms of its nature, and is more perfect and stronger in some others. A being that has no cause has priority in existence compared to others, and is by definition prior to all other beings. By the same token, the existence of each one of the active intellects has a priority over the existence of other intellects, and the existence of substance is prior to the existence of accident. (*Asfār*, i. 1. 36).

The principle of gradation culminates in a view of metaphysics that sees everything as a symphony of infinite modalities and manifestations of one single being and reality. While existence remains unaffected by its various manifestations, it creates different orders of reality each possessing a different degree of truth. This is further underlined by the 'ontological simplicity of existence' according to which existence as an absolutely simple reality permeates the entire spectrum of existence. In Ṣadrā's words: '...What exists in the external world is nothing other than the one, all-penetrating existence, and there is nothing in the abode of existence except the One who maintains His pure oneness and is above any mixing up with contingent and created beings.' (*Īqāẓ*, 50)

Ṣadrā's axiological ontology states that existence not only generates things but also saturates them with meaning. Contrary to subject-centred epistemologies, the human mind does not assign meaning to particular beings based on generalizations and abstractions. The mind is capable of creating meaning out of relations and proportions that it observes in things. It can also generate new meanings by using concepts and notions. But meaning is not the exclusive property of the mind. Nor is it the result of the internal procedures of the knowing subject. Ṣadrā rejects these definitions as remnants of a subjectivist epistemology which results from a fundamental failure to ground epistemic concepts in a proper ontology. Rather, meaning is a function of existence and emerges from the self-disclosure and self-delimitation of existence:

> It is certain that existence allows intensification and diminution, and whatever is strong in existence becomes more inclusive and encompassing of universal meanings and disembodied intellective quiddities. When existence reaches the level of the simple intellect, which is completely disengaged from the world of corporeal bodies and quantities, it becomes all of the *intelligibilia* and all things in a manner more virtuous and noble than whatever they are based upon. Whoever has not tasted this path cannot understand the simple intellect, which is the source of all detailed knowledge. (*Asfār*, i. 3. 373–74)

Ṣadrā's grand project of grounding all things in existence leads to the revision of the main issues of traditional philosophy. As we shall see in the next chapter, Ṣadrā's mature thought is an application of his single fundamental insight about the centrality of existence and the ontological symphony of its modalities. Ṣadrā does not defend ontological monism at the expense of cosmological pluralism and vice versa. Instead, he works with a set of metaphysical principles that evade any simplistic categorizations and urge us to both experience the ever-dynamic nature of existence and provide a coherent account of its conceptual representation. Applied to the main issues of traditional philosophy, the principle of existence presents a radically different world-picture and the place of the human state in it.

4

Synthesis: Transcendent Wisdom and the Great Chain of Being

The key ideas of Ṣadrā's Transcendent Wisdom follow logically from the all-inclusive and dynamic reality of existence and give us a fairly unified and integrated view of the cosmos. The ultimate goal of the Transcendent Wisdom is to illustrate the proper means of understanding the relationship between God, the natural world and the human state so that mortal humans can realize the destiny for which they have been created. As we shall see, this forms the basis of Ṣadrā's notion of philosophy as spiritual anthropology. Furthermore, since reality is multilayered and dynamic, the methods proper to understand it must also be multidimensional and integral. Ontological reductionism is a philosophical error because it makes reality less than what it is and creates the illusion that the intrinsic complexity of the order of existence can be explained away through abstract categories and schematic taxonomies.

A fundamental principle of Ṣadrean metaphysics is the notion that all beings have two faces, one pointing to themselves, the other to something beyond. Considered in themselves, beings have an existence of their own and are complete and self-sufficient. They exist as self-regulating entities within the matrix of causal relations. But since there is no effect without a cause and infinite regression cannot be an explanation for the existence of things, there is no existent without an agent that generates it. Infinite regression, i.e., the explanation that A is caused by B, B is caused by C, *ad infinitum,* is not a plausible explanation because it explains only a series of causes and effects, not the reason *why* they exist. As Wittgenstein famously said in his *Tractatus*, all explanations must come to an end in something that terminates the infinite series of the cause–effect chain. This higher principle must contain in itself its own *raison d'etre*. It must be a principle in which both the *how* and *why* questions are answered. For Ṣadrā, only God can fulfill these conditions.

In the language of philosophy, God is both the 'First Cause' (*al-sabab al-awwal*) and the 'Cause of causes' (*sabab al-asbāb*). God is the ultimate cause in the ontological and theological senses of the term. In this regard, beings have another, more fundamental face turned towards their Creator. 'Every being has a special face turned towards God, the Lord of lords, the Cause of causes' (*Īqāẓ*, 59). Considered in relation to God, beings have no existence of their own and cannot claim self-sufficiency. They exist to the extent to which God grants them existence out of His mercy. It is in this sense that Ibn ʿArabī says that 'existence is mercy'. The Qurʾān says that God is 'abundantly rich' (*al-ghaniyy*) whereas the world of creation is in a state of absolute 'indigence' (*al-faqr*) towards Him. Only God can be said to exist properly; all else is derived existence – a shadow, a speck in the infinite ocean of God's creative power.

This onto-theological premise, shared by the monotheistic religions, leads to what we might call a 'metaphysics of binary relations' whereby things are ontologically intertwined with their opposites. Dualities inform the basic function of things in the universe: existence and essence, meaning and form, substance and accident, cause and effect, necessity and contingency, invisible and visible, and so on. This long list of binaries underlies Ṣadrean as well as traditional Islamic metaphysics. Quoting from Ghazālī's *Mishkāt al-anwār*, Ṣadrā notes that all beings are known by their opposites. We may extend this to the relationship between God and everything else and assume that God and creation represent a binary opposition.

This conclusion, however, is flawed because what is infinite and absolute cannot be compared to what is finite and relative. Even if we accept that there is a duality between God and His creation, this does not justify dualism because God and created beings are not on the same ontological level. God is above all opposites, dualisms and binaries. His absolute unity transcends the multiplicity of the created order. Plurality of forms is a reality but only in a relative sense and cannot be a principle on its own. Behind the multiplicity of various substances and forms lies an underlying unity pointing to the singular reality of existence. 'Unity-in-multiplicity' (*al-waḥda fī l-kathrā*) is the presiding principle which grounds fundamental metaphysics. For Ṣadrā, this is the *sine qua non* of metaphysics without which we end up with a fragmented ontology and disjointed cosmology.

THE METAPHYSICS OF THE ONE

One of the goals of metaphysics is, then, to overcome the dualities and multiplicities of the visible phenomena and uncover their essential, underlying unity. The unity of existence, which Ṣadrā adopts from the school of Ibn ᶜArabī, already indicates the direction of metaphysics as a unifying enterprise. But for Ṣadrā, this unity is not something superimposed upon existence. Rather, it emerges from the essential identity of existence and the nature of things. As we saw in our discussion of Ṣadrā's ontology, existence is a single, unitary reality that maintains its unity while giving rise to a cosmic symphony of colours, forms and modalities. Rather than taking the multiplicity of things at their face value and treating them as self-grounding and self-regulating entities, Ṣadrā aims to go beyond appearances and see the underlying unity underneath them. This unity, however, is to be sought not in the things themselves, as the pre-Socratic philosophers attempted to do with such ethereal entities as fire, air or water, but in the higher principle which generates them.

The perspective of unity which underpins Ṣadrā's Transcendent Wisdom is in tune with the Islamic notion of Divine unity (*tawḥīd*). Islam's robust monotheism penetrates everything from science and art to jurisprudence and politics. Philosophy is no exception. The Islamic intellectual tradition has considered God's absolute oneness as a logical necessity and also as a presiding principle that gives meaning, purpose and structure to the universe. An important component of this view of the cosmos is the premise that the realm of existence is 'one', not in the numerical sense but in the sense that everything is related to everything else through a higher point of reference. In Ṣadrā's words, 'verily, the abode of existence is one and the entire universe is one big living being [in which] everything is related to everything else' (*Asfār*, ii. 2. 342). Al-Fārābī concurs when he describes the world of existence as 'one single living being'.[1] It is this wholeness and unity that establishes a relationship of complementarity and harmony between the natural and human worlds.

This cosmological outlook, largely lost since the European Enlightenment, defines the universe as a 'macrocosm' and the human being as a 'microcosm'. The universe as the macrocosm denotes a state of universal order; the human being as the microcosm refers to his connection to this universal order. The universe is 'a big man' and man 'a small universe'. Ṣadrā takes this a step further and posits man and nature as constitutive of each other in terms of their meaning and purpose:

All existence from its highest to the lowest and from its lowest to the highest is [united] in a single relationship by which some parts of it are related to some others. Everything is united in spite of their external diversity. Their unity is not like the conjunction of corporeal bodies whereby their goals are conjoined and their surfaces linked. Rather, the whole universe is one single animate being (*ḥayawān wāḥid*) just like a single soul, and its active potencies are like the intelligences, the souls and the like as the potencies of a single soul... man is the last being with which the world of nature is sealed... in man are gathered the truths of the higher and lower worlds and it is he who has added to the total truth of the world the truths of the True One from His Names and Qualities with which man's great vicegerency in the macro-cosmos is affirmed after his lesser vicegerency in the world of nature. (*Asfār*, ii. 2. 349–50)

Ṣadrā describes the world of existence as pointing to God's oneness, wisdom, power and generosity. The essential unity between the multiple realms of existence creates a context in which man's horizon joins that of the universe and 'moves you from one station to another and elevates you from one

1 al-Farabi, *K. al-Milla wa-nuṣuṣ ukhra* (ed. Muḥsin Mahdi, 1991), 65–6.

level to another whereby you gain the true faith and correct belief regarding your origin...' (*Asfār*, ii. 2. 348).

The order in the universe is underlined and sustained by the principle of 'intellect' (*al-ʿaql*) inherent in the things themselves. Given the enormous complexity and sophistication of the universe and the rule-bound way in which it functions, the universe is 'reason incarnate', to use Einstein's phrase, in that the laws of nature that govern the life of the universe reflect the intrinsic intelligibility of things. In another respect, the world of existence oscillates between perfection and imperfection, between existence and non-existence. The extremely diverse aspects of the universe must be united by some underlying principle; otherwise it descends into chaos. But we know through empirical evidence and intuition that the universe is an ordered being. That is why it has been called 'cosmos' rather than chaos. It is no coincidence that the word cosmos means both 'world' and 'order'. We cannot have a world without an inherent order in it. What establishes order and harmony between the various degrees and realms of existence is the 'intellect':

> There must be some perfect being in existence to mediate between what lies above perfection and what is imperfect, and it is the intellect. If an imperfect being had emanated from God in the first place, and since He is above even perfection, then the relationship between that which comes about through effusion and its source would be lost. (*Asfār*, iii. 2. 272)

Ṣadrā holds that the ontological order of the universe requires a robust causality in both horizontal and vertical directions. In this double sense, causality explains not only relations between cause and effect but also and more importantly the ontological dependency of the latter on the former and ties everything to its origin:

Everything that happens in the universe happens for a reason. Thus whatever is not necessitated [through a causal link] cannot exist. The chain of causes goes back to a single principle which causes beings [to exist] through its knowledge, wisdom and providence for them. There is nothing in existence which negates the nature of its reasons and causes that lead to the True One [as the ultimate Cause of causes]. In fact, the caused corresponds to its cause and even emanates from it. Therefore what appear to be contradictory movements [events, things in nature] are in reality all unified and orderly in regards to the totality of the universe. (*Asfār*, iii. 2. 112)

THE PROBLEM OF CREATION

While the order of the universe can be rationally understood and intuitively perceived, there is an element of mystery underlying it. The mystery is contained in the perennial question of why there is something rather than nothing. From a creationist point of view, the question can be reformulated as why God decided to create in the first place. The question is an important one given the common theistic tenet that creation neither adds to nor subtracts from the infinite perfection of God. If God is perfect without the world, why did He decide to create it?

Volition versus necessity

This question has been answered mainly in two ways, which we may call 'necessitarian' and 'libertarian'. According to the necessitarian school, God creates out of necessity in the sense that a perfect and infinitely good being cannot be conceived of existing only for itself. To use the language of Plato, the good cannot not give of itself. The *Timaeus* (29 30) lays the foundations of the necessitarian paradigm of creation: 'Let me tell you then why the creator made this world of generation. He was good, and the good can never have any jealousy of anything. And being free from jealousy, he desired that all things should be as like himself as they could be. This is in the truest sense the origin of creation and of the world... the deeds of the best could never be or have been other than the fairest...'

Being infinitely good and gracious, God cannot be so jealous as not to allow anything else besides Him to exist. The necessitarian view thus constrains God in His choice of creation, arguing that God had to create in the first place out of His infinite perfection and goodness. God cannot go against His own nature which obliges him to give of Himself. Even though this appears to jeopardize God's omnipotence and will, it argues against an arbitrary, whimsical deity and secures the essential intelligibility of the order of existence.

The proponents of this view argue for a kind of Divine determinism whereby God does not have the choice not to create. As the medieval philosophers insist, however, this is not a necessity imposed upon God from outside. Creation as 'emanation' or 'pouring forth' is not a material or natural necessity whereby God is forced to act by a set of conditions external to Himself. Rather, this is an internal necessity, an intrinsic determinism that makes sense only within the purview of the Divine itself. It is the Divine nature that generates this necessity.

While the necessitarian school insists on the self-binding condition of God's nature, the libertarian or 'voluntaristic' school conceives creation as a free and voluntary act of God with no necessities involved. God creates because he chooses to, and there is no further explanation to be offered. Since all explanations eventually come to an end, God's will terminates all causal chains. God's will to create must, then, be accepted as the final answer to the question of why there is something rather than nothing.

Ṣadrā took a middle way between the two alternatives. He argued that neither God's nature nor His will should be sacrificed. Will, let alone God's will, is not devoid of wisdom and intelligence, for willing something is predicated upon certain conditions. An agent who wills should also know what he is willing and anticipate its consequences. He should have an understanding of what he wants. He should see what his will means for others. And finally, he should make a decision to want one thing rather than something else, and so on.

Ṣadrā concludes that God must know what he wills when He decides to create. Since God's will never contradicts His nature, God wills through knowledge and wisdom. For our philosopher, this is a sufficient argument to overcome the seeming contradiction between necessity and volition as far as God's act of creation is concerned.

The essential createdness of the world

How is the world related to God? Before answering this question, which has caused numerous problems for theologians and philosophers over the centuries, Ṣadrā reiterates that the world has been created not only temporally but also essentially. Ṣadrā calls those who hold this view 'the people of truth and certainty' and sees them in perfect harmony with 'saints and those who are deep in knowledge and who take their light from the niche of the prophecy of the perfect prophets' (*Ḥudūth*, 18). He notes that the temporal createdness of the world is the key belief of Jews, Christians and Muslims in the sense that the world as that which is other than God, His Names and Qualities is temporally originated, i.e., it is an existent after having been non-existent. This 'after-ness' is a real after-ness and real temporality, not just essential posteriority. The world is in need of something prior to it in its own essence as this is the case for everything contingent from the point of view of its essential origination (*ḥuduth dhātī*). [Such a being] substantiates neither existence nor non-existence by itself. (*Ḥudūth*, 16)

Some philosophical schools uphold the eternity of the world as a logical premise and cannot prove its temporal origination unless another set of arguments is introduced. Ṣadrā argues that the idea of the eternity of the world began after Aristotle and this was a major breach of the tradition of the Greeks themselves. It is also against the belief of the three Abrahamic faiths. Ṣadrā calls this mediocre 'philosophy based on conjecture... in which truth and falsehood are mixed together' (*Ḥudūth*, 14). But 'faith is different from certainty' and as a light from God, the 'path to certainty is either through demonstration or intuition through inspiration' (*Ḥudūth*, 9). No matter how sound it is, however, philosophical demonstration alone is not enough to yield certainty in such a matter as the creation of the world; one needs the guidance of revelation and the light of prophetic philosophy. Ṣadrā argues that the Muslim Peripatetics' ontology and cosmology had led them to believing in the temporal origination of the world while maintaining its eternal coexistence with God.

Ṣadrā insists instead on the 'essential origination' of the world as opposed to its mere 'temporal origination' because the former makes the world absolutely contingent and originated while the latter does so only partially and leaves too much independence for the world. Ṣadrā's goal is to move from *time* to *essence* to prove the utter dependence of the world on its Creator. 'Origination' signifies an essential dimension of created things whereby they are preceded by non-existence. 'The essential origination is that the existence of something is not dependent upon itself by itself but upon something else whether this dependence is specific to a particular time, continuous in all times or above the horizon of time and motion' (*Asfār*, iii. 3. 249).

Since all beings are both essentially and temporally originated, the divine act of creation permeates all beings and saturates them with meaning and purpose. The mystery of existence penetrates everything: 'There is nothing in the universe whose root does not come from a Divine reality, and in it you find a Divine mystery' (*Īqāẓ*, 35). The order, harmony and regularity of the universe does not cancel bur rather confirms God's direct agency because 'the real effective agent in all [of the universe] is God, the Transcendent' (*Asfār*, 8. 223). God's presence or immanence in the world introduces a dynamic relationship between the Creator and the created and denies the world of existence any claim to being self-grounded. This ontological-cum-theological premise enables Ṣadrā to develop a 'vitalistic' cosmology, as we shall see shortly, and leads him to a fundamental critique of Aristotelian cosmology based on fixed substances and an eternally existing universe. It also makes it possible to dispense with the emanationist model of creation because Ṣadrā's gradational ontology and the self-effusion of existence renders emanation redundant: God acts with both wisdom and will. He creates both directly and through intermediaries.

COSMOLOGY AND THE NATURAL ORDER

As a manifestation of the multiple modalities of existence, Ṣadrā's universe is thoroughly teleological, i.e., has 'purpose' (*ghāya*) as part of its existential constitution.

Everything in nature is directed towards a 'universal purpose' which makes it complete. While each species or genus has its own specific *telos* towards which it moves, the cosmos as a whole has purposiveness built into it. The ever-continuous 'intensification' (*tashaddud*) of the order of nature comes about as a result of the self-effusion (*fayḍ*) of existence. In this regard, the universe displays a dual nature: on one hand, it subsists by the Divine Imperative 'Be!' (*kun, esto*). Nothing moves without God's command and no being can claim to possess a reality on its own. This applies to all causal relations and changes as well. On the other hand, however, God has created the world in such a way that it possesses a strict regularity and constancy. The universe exists as an ordered reality because it contains some intrinsic principles that secure its regularity. Ṣadrā sees no contradiction between the two orders of reality and takes horizontal and vertical causalities to be complementary.

This, however, was not the commonly accepted position of the Muslim theologians. The Islamic occasionalists, especially the Ashʿaris, felt they had to defend vertical causality at the expense of horizontal causality in order to leave room for miracles. Ṣadrā, being aware of occasionalism's inconsistencies, defined the two lines of causality as in perfect accord in that God sustains the world of creation in such a way that it is bound to be causal and rule-governed. The great chain of being is thus construed as a unified structure that allows for a self-regulating dynamism on the one hand, and the perpetual presence of the creative act of God, on the other.

To explain, among other things, the binary relationship between the two types of causality, Ṣadrā introduced a novel concept called 'substantial motion' (*al-ḥarakāt al-jawhariyya*) and used it to establish 'change-in-substance' as an intrinsic quality of things. Instead of defining motion and change as a system of external relations taking place only in the category of accident, he posited substantial motion as an essential property of the way things are. A far cry from an atomistic and mechanical cosmos, this notion turns the universe into an abode of change and permanence, renewal and continuity all at once.

SUBSTANTIAL MOTION

The doctrine of substantial motion is based on the premise that everything undergoes substantial change and transformation as a result of the self-flow and 'penetration of existence' (*sarayān al-wujūd*). In contrast to Aristotle and Ibn Sīnā who had accepted change only in the four categories of quantity, quality, position and place, Ṣadrā defines change as an all-pervasive reality running through the entire cosmos including the category of substance.

His argument for introducing change into substance, which was not possible within the confines of Aristotelian physics, is that change in the accidental qualities of physical bodies has to come from their substance because accidents do not have an existence independent of the substance to which they are attached. In fact, every accidental change is the result of a deeper change that takes place in the substance of things. This holds true even for positional movement, i.e., when the object A moves from point B to point C. Ṣadrā calls this type of motion 'accidental' and describes it as 'movement-in-movement'. Every accidental change, which is immediately accessible to our five senses, can be traced back to substantial motion. Substantial motion is, then, an intrinsic feature of things, and since every positional movement, which we take to be the measure of time, is ultimately a modulation of substantial movement, time should be redefined in tandem with the existential transformation of physical substances. Furthermore, since the celestial spheres, whose circular movement the Peripatetics had taken to be the primary measure of time, are themselves subject to substantial motion, we can no longer turn to them for the measure of linear time. Ṣadrā thus transforms all existing substances into beings whose 'quiddity is stable and whose existence is continuously changing'. This makes all beings in the universe a 'continuum of events' rather than opaque, unchanging physical structures. 'Relations' rather than solidified objects populate Ṣadrā's cosmological scheme.

Ṣadrā made use of substantial motion to explain, among others, the temporal origination of the world. If everything in the cosmos is in constant change and in a different mode of existence at every moment, then it is always different from what it was before and will be different at the next instance of its existentiation. This suggests that every physical being is 'preceded by non-existence', and such an order of being, taken as a whole, can neither subsist by itself nor can be eternal. The physical world must be temporally originated and renewed at every successive phase of its existential transformation. What makes this existential transformation possible is not an external agent that acts upon the world of nature antecedently but 'nature' (*ṭabīʿa*) in a particularly Ṣadrean sense. Nature here signifies the immediate cause of movement and transformation in physical bodies. As the word 'nature' in English suggests, it also denotes an ontological state of inclination towards the final goal of particular beings. Beings contain 'nature' as a principle of both change and continuity. Insofar as the physical transformation of things is concerned, nature acts as a principle of change. However, insofar as the preservation of natural forms is concerned, nature functions as a principle of continuity and permanence. Ṣadrā explains this dual function of nature as follows:

There is no doubt that every material substance has a continuously changing nature on the one hand, and an enduring and unchanging structure on the other. The relation between the two aspects is similar to the relation between the body and the soul. While the body is in constant change and flow, the human soul endures because it preserves its identity by the passing on of essential forms in an uninterrupted continuous process. (*Asfār*, i. 1. 3)

Nature is directly related to substantial motion and essential change:

The immediate cause of motion has to be something with a stable essence and continuously changing being... the immediate cause of all kinds of motion is not other than nature. This nature is the substance by which things subsist and become actualized as a species [i.e., as a particular entity]. This refers to the first perfection of natural things insofar as they are actual beings [in the external world]. Therefore it is concluded and established from this [consideration] that every physical being is a continuously changing entity with a flowing and fluid identity despite the fact that its quiddity is impervious to change. (*Asfār*, iii. 1. 62)

The order and regularity that we see in the natural world is a function of this principle of nature. The physical architecture of the universe is based on precise principles and thus cannot be explained by 'chance': 'Chances... are neither constant nor dominant [in nature] whereas order in nature is both dominant and continuous. There is nothing in nature that happens by chance or haphazardly... Everything in nature is directed towards some universal purpose' (*Asfār*, iii. 1. 49).

A fluid world-order

The principle of substantial motion turns the world-order into a continuously changing structure based on patterns of essential change and continuity, and replaces the Aristotelian universe of fixed substances with processes of change and renewal (*Asfār*, i. 3. 128 ff.). This is underlined by the dynamic nature of the 'expanding existence' (*al-wujūd al-munbasiṭ*), which constantly seeks to return to its point of origin. The ultimate agent of change is existence but since existence is the principle of *both* change and permanence, the universe displays them without contradiction. To explain why the essential nature of things remains the same, Ṣadrā turns to the doctrine of Platonic Forms according to which the 'intellective existence of things and their separate Platonic Forms are eternally the same in God's knowledge' (*Ḥudūth*, 58). Combining the language of temporal and ontological causality, he further adds that

> Both demonstrative proof and the Qurʾān establish that this corporeal world as a whole is originated and preceded by temporal non-existence. Natural entities have no enduring subsistence (*baqāʾ*) because they are never devoid of temporal origination; and whatever is not devoid of temporal origination has an identity that is originated with a gradual essence and changing constitution. But the truth of the species has an unchanging existence in God's knowledge. (*Maẓāhir*, 67)

Ṣadrā's defence of change as an essential nature of things lies at the heart of his attempt to relate the 'temporally originated' to the 'eternal' (*rabṭ al-ḥadīth bi-l-qadīm*). Ṣadrā tries to link the two orders of reality in a way that would not harm the eternal unity and absoluteness of the Creator. As he puts it, 'there is no harm in assuming that from God's making comes the existence of a substance by which happenings and renewals emanate from God the Exalted who is above any change. Accordingly, this substance must have infinite potency in actual effects in a continuous manner' (*Asfār*, iii. 2. 121). Ṣadrā's goal is to establish change as the essence of *all* things so that he can account for change in the world of creation without having this change reflect upon the Creator.

Substantial motion breaks with the main thrust of Peripatetic physics and cosmology and turns the present world-order into a constant state of flow. Ṣadrā argues that the first to speak of perennial change as a constituent element of the physical world is God's revealed book. He quotes a number of verses including *al-Naml*, 27: 88, *al-Qāf*, 50: 15, *al-Furqān*, 25: 59 and *al-Sajda*, 32: 4 to exemplify the fluid nature of the corporeal universe (*Ḥudūth*, 59–60). This is important because Ṣadrā wants to reduce both change and permanence to one single principle: existence. This is not 'existence' in a generic sense but 'existence in expansion' unveiling itself in various modalities and states. To illustrate how this change-in-continuity happens, he refers to the difference between soul and character. While the soul remains the same, the character is 'something in constant flow and renewal'. The totality of the two, however, gives us a unified entity called the human person: 'Everyone feels himself to be one single person without change even though it is one through the conjunction [of successive states] throughout the lapse of one's life' (*Ḥudūth*, 69).

Ṣadrā finds the Peripatetics' explanation of quantitative change unsatisfactory because it fails to account for the continuously successive stages of change. The Peripatetics subscribe to a softened version of the generation and corruption argument, which accounts for radical change rather than gradual transformation. It was this confusion that had led Suhrawardī to reject quantitative change altogether (*Ḥudūth*,

77). Ibn Sīnā, too, was frustrated with the whole issue of quantitative change. After spending a good deal of time on change in the *Shifā*ʾ, he admits that the issue is far from being resolved.[1]

Why did this lead to a major problem? Because Aristotelian ontology-cum-cosmology which the Muslim Peripatetics accepted was too opaque to explain the internal dynamism of existence and its modalities. Following the Peripatetics, Suhrawardī had taken substances to be solid objects that can accept only accidents without themselves being amenable to change (*Asfār*, i. 3. 89–90). But this gives us a one-dimensional ontology and a static world-order, which follows the Aristotelian notion that only the unchanging substances can account for the order and structure of the physical world.

By employing his concept of existence, Ṣadrā rejects this static ontology on the grounds that it fails to provide a philosophically cogent and theologically appropriate explanation of how the created is related to the Creator without harming God's absolute oneness. In addition to several general arguments, Ṣadrā gives the example of substances with certain accidents. When we look at a black object, for instance, what we have is something black 'which is a single identity through a single conjunction from the first state of its intensification to its ultimate point' (*Ḥudūth*, 69; see also *Asfār*, i. 3. 128–37). He takes this to be a generic property of existence qualified by such modalities as 'blackness'. In this strongly ontological view, not only substances but also accidents become modalities of existence. Instead of saying that 'a black object exists', Ṣadrā would have us say that 'existence-as-black-object' has such-and-such qualities.

---

1 Ibn Sīnā, *Shifā*ʾ, *Ṭabīʿiyyāt* (1960), 195.

In a clearly Platonic fashion, entities retain their essential identities through their eternal forms in God. Things as particular beings never remain the same; they seek to attain their 'final differentia', which makes the physical universe a constantly changing and dynamic order. But their intellective substance, i.e., Platonic Form, is permanently the same in God's knowledge: 'These intellective substances are like the rays and glimpses of the First Single Light, for they are the forms of what is in God's knowledge. They do not have an existence independent of God; they are beings whose essences are intimately related to the First Reality' (*Ḥuduth*, 81).

As the principle of change and permanence, existence serves as the ultimate link between the absolutely unchanging God and the continuously changing world. That is why the study of existence is an exercise in both ontology and theology. Grasping the truth and reality of existence is a way of participating in the higher principle that generates and sustains it. In Ibn ʿArabī's words, 'existence... is finding the Truth (*wijdān al-ḥaqq*) in ecstasy (*al-wajd*)'. Existence is crucial for both cosmology and metaphysics because 'the existence of the Truth in ecstasy is commensurate with the Divine Name, which it contemplates, and the Divine Names ultimately belong to the Truth itself'.[1] It is in reference to this 'secret' that Ṣadrā says that 'the particular existence for everything is its principle; and it is particularized by itself. While remaining one, it may possess various states and degrees. In each state and degree, it has universal and essential properties. While maintaining its oneness, it possesses different meanings abstracted from it and united with it through the kind of unification that comes about because of its change in various

1 Ibn ʿArabī, *al-Futūḥāt al-Makkiyya* (1997), iii. (ch. 237), 527.

states of transformation' (*Ḥudūth*, 83). Ṣadrā ends his discussion by saying that one can attain this state of understanding only through a 'second nature', viz., by assuming a different outlook on things.

Relating God to the world

The way God is related to the world is similar to the way existence is related to its various modalities. In Ṣadrā's cosmo-temporal language, this refers to three types of temporality and three levels of existence:

> In the language of the pillars of wisdom, the relation of the unchanging to the unchanging is *sarmad* ('perpetuity'), the unchanging to the changing is *dahr* ('eternity'), and the changing to the changing is *zamān* ('time'). What they mean by the first is the relation of God to His Names, Qualities and knowledge. By the second, they mean the relation of His unchanging knowledge to His continuously renewing contents of knowledge, which are the existents of this world through an existential togetherness. By the third, they mean the relation of some of the continuously renewing contents of His knowledge to some others through temporal togetherness, which is itself the temporal antecedence and precedence. Ponder on this! (*Ḥudūth*, 130)

Creation is not something God 'does' like a mechanical or disinterested agent. God acts with wisdom and purpose but also with love and affection. This is where the utterly transcendent God discloses Himself through a loving act of creation. The intellective forms of things, which Plato and his followers called the 'divine similes', form an intimate relationship between God and His creation. What makes creation meaningful is not its physical qualities such as quantity, quality or position, but its intelligible substance because 'these intellective forms, illuminative similes and divine forms of knowledge are eternally tied to their Agent; and their purpose is to contemplate the beauty of their source and creator' (*Ḥudūth*, 140). The *mysterium tremendum* is revealed in both love and knowledge because 'no one can deny the existence of Divine love and affection in these separate forms since... the love of that which is higher is embedded firmly in that which is lower' (*Ḥudūth*, 141).

In conclusion, God reveals himself in His creation through the degrees and stages of descent. God creates both *things* and the *principles* by which they exist. Ṣadrā sums up this point with a historical overview:

> The Divine Essence has rays, lights, glimpses and effects. Existence is nothing but a dawning of His light and a ray of His manifestation. The majority of the philosophers have called these rays and lights 'active intellects'. The Peripatetics, who are the followers of the First Teacher, call them 'forms of knowledge' which subsist with His Essence. Plato and his followers call them 'illuminative similes'. The majority of the *mutakallimūn* call them states and the Sufis sometime call them names and sometimes fixed essences (*al-aʿyān al-thābita*). (*Ḥudūth*, 144)

These illuminative substances are essential to explain why the world has meaning. For our philosopher, the world of creation is meaningful because God has created it, and God, the Qurʾān says, does nothing in vain (*Āl ʿImrān*, 3: 191). But the world is also meaningful because it moves towards a higher purpose, a *telos*, which relates all of its discrete parts to one another. The intrinsic meaning and intelligibility which Ṣadrā attributes to the world of creation is not something superadded to it a posteriori. Rather, it is ingrained in the way things exist. Thus the world is meaningful for a third reason: its intrinsic structures and internal relations themselves are structures of meaning. By establishing a strong axiological link between creation and existence, Ṣadrā advocates a strong version of axiarchism and proposes a new ontology of meaning:

> The house of your heart has now been enlightened by the light of the sun of the truth from the firmament of the sacred intellect. You also believe that the purpose of the will of the spheres, the movement of the celestial bodies and the flow of the universe as it is is that all of this be good and blissful. The source of creation is the existence of God and His effulgence. The soul's attainment of the degree of the intellect is its repose and its final stage whereby there is continuous restfulness and perfect satisfaction.
>
> This is the final goal of the making of the universe, the rule of the spheres, the movement of the celestial spheres, the coming of the prophets and messengers, and the descent of angels from the heavens with revelation and messages. The purpose of all of this is such that the whole universe will be good; evil and imperfection will cease in it; it will return to where it began and will be (re-) attached with it; wisdom will be completed and creation will be perfected; the world of generation and corruption will come to an end; the world will be extinguished; the great day of reckoning will arrive; evil and its people will be effaced; disbelief and its party will perish; falsehood will become null and void; and the Truth will be realized through Its words and signs. This is the ultimate goal and the supreme knowledge. (*Ḥudūth*, 145–6)

KNOWLEDGE AND EXISTENCE

What kind of an epistemology emerges once we move from an ontology of fixed substances to a metaphysics of existence as developed by Ṣadrā? Since existence is the source of all perceptual properties and axiological terms, our framework of analysis for knowledge must reflect its basic reality. Knowledge is our mental-intellectual access to the reality of things and unveils the different modalities of existence. But what aspects of existence can we grasp through empirical and conceptual knowledge? If a notion of knowledge based on existence produces an epistemology that de-centres the knowing subject, what is the role of the human person in cognitive experience? What are the criteria for reliable knowledge? Where do we place the function of knowledge in the larger scheme of things? Ṣadrā's being-centred epistemology provides some stimulating answers to these questions. After a careful analysis of ontological and epistemological terms, Ṣadrā makes his radical claim: knowledge is identical with existence.

Ṣadrā's concept of knowledge weaves together his ontology, cosmology and psychology. He incorporates many elements from the Peripatetic and Illuminationist schools. Like Ibn Sīnā, he defines 'demonstrative knowledge' (*burhān*) as based on sound proofs, obtained through the careful analysis of logical concepts. He also accepts Ibn Sīnā's notion of 'intuition' (*ḥads*) as 'quick and immediate apprehension' and posits it as the ultimate basis of self-evident truths that cannot be further derived from other propositions. In this sense, knowledge is 'constructed' through logical demonstration on the one hand, and 'discovered' through intuitive perception on the other. But he criticizes the Peripatetic philosophers for defining knowledge as 'abstraction' or 'disembodiment' (*tajarrud*), i.e., the abstraction of intelligible forms from actually existing things. Such a definition of knowledge leads to something less than the reality of things, for abstraction implies 'leaving out' certain properties of things and carrying only some mental attributes to the mind. The epistemic that the theory of 'abstraction' creates between the knower and the known leads to ignorance, not knowledge.

Knowledge is existence

To overcome the difficulties of reducing knowledge to mental abstraction, Ṣadrā turns to his gradational ontology and subsumes all knowledge under existence. This is how he develops his arguments. When we say we know something, we affirm or deny the existence of something, and this 'something' is *ultimately* nothing but a modality of existence. In simpler forms of cognition, we always perceive an aspect of existence. When I say that I see the door at the end of the room or that I know that it is raining outside, I am simply referring to different modalities of existence appearing as room, door, rain, etc. To use Ṣadrā's heavily ontological language, there is no such thing as 'door' and 'rain' but rather 'existence-particularized-as-door', 'existence-particularized-as-rain', and so on. This suggests that my knowing *of* something is always mediated through existence and its modalities. The ultimate object of knowledge is thus existence particularized through a myriad of modes and states. It is in this sense that knowledge is 'a mode of existence' (*naḥw al-wujūd*).

Ṣadrā criticizes most *kalām* thinkers, particularly Fakhr al-Dīn al-Rāzī, for defining knowledge as a 'relation' (*iḍāfa*) between the knower and the known. When we define knowledge as a relation, we deprive both the knowing subject and the object known of any cognitive content *before* their epistemic encounter. But this cannot be true, says Ṣadrā, because existence is intrinsically saturated with meaning and intelligibility whether a subject knows it or not. Furthermore, to know something is to grasp and 'appropriate' its intelligible form. Intelligible forms are not mere concepts, notions or contents of the mind. Rather, they are substances that belong to the world of the *intelligibilia*. To quote Ṣadrā, 'material forms are nothing but icons and moulds of these disembodied [i.e., intelligible] forms' (*Asfār*, i. 3. 304). Since the Ideas or 'intelligible forms' exist in an immutable world above the world of generation and corruption, they possess universality and permanence: 'The forms of particular entities are universal, general truths existing in the world of God's command and predestination' (*Asfār*, iv. 1. 126). Because of their higher ontological status, intelligible forms are cognitively more reliable and enduring than the senses. The 'form', i.e., the idea of the horse, for instance, is more 'real' than the physical horse. An individual horse may have different qualities, decay, become sick or die, but the idea of the horse or what Ṣadrā, following the Platonists, calls the 'intellective horse' remains stable and constant:

These forms [i.e., the archetypal forms] are more exalted and noble than what is to be found in lower existents. This animal in flesh, composed of contradictory qualities and forms in constant change, is a parable and shadow for the simple animal while there is still a higher [animal] above it. Now, this is the intellective animal which is simple, singular, and containing in its simplicity all of the individual instances and classes of material and mental existence under its species. And this is its universal archetype, i.e., the intellective horse. This holds true for all species of animals and other existents. (*Asfār*, i. 3. 304)

This suggests that the senses can help us know the *physical properties* of things. However, it is the intellect that uncovers the *meaning* of things by reaching out to the world of intelligible forms. In knowing things, we participate in their intelligible reality and, by derivation, in the world of immutable ideas and intelligible forms. This is underlined by another principle of epistemology that goes back to Aristotle – a principle that defines incorporeality and disembodiment as a condition of intelligibility. An existent is closer to being intelligible to the extent to which it is removed from material conditions and lends itself to have meaning-properties. Things are more 'real' when they are closer to their 'formal' reality, i.e., the intellective form, and the intellective form obtains only when it goes beyond the limitations of corporeal existence. Sensate beings perceived through sensation have a limited range of meaning-properties whereas higher beings, since they are removed from corporeal existence, possess a greater range of intelligible forms and meanings. Sensate forms appear to be more real because they are immediately available to our five senses. But in reality, the intelligible forms are more real because they contain more meanings and valuational terms.

UNITY OF THE INTELLECT AND THE INTELLIGIBLE

This ontological grounding of cognitive and epistemic terms in existence turns knowledge into an act of 'participation' and moves it beyond the subjective competencies of the knowing mind. Ṣadrā defends this thesis through the notorious argument of the 'unification of the intellect and the intelligible' (*ittiḥād al-ʿāqil wa-l-maʿqūl*). As a recurring theme in Ṣadrā, the argument states that when reason or intellect knows something, it becomes one and the same with it. Since the 'ideas' or 'intelligible forms' which the mind comes to know are 'real', i.e., have a real ontological basis in the world of actualities, this unification denotes an ontological act on the part of the knowing mind. Knowledge as unification is also knowledge as participation in the intelligible form of things. This is an act of self-overcoming in that the mind, reason or the intellect goes beyond itself and reaches to something not encapsulated by the mind. This non-subjectivist concept of knowing is a logical result of Ṣadrā's being-centred metaphysics and forms the backbone of his epistemology.

Ibn Sīnā and Suhrawardī were opposed to any unification between the intellect and what it knows. Ibn Sīnā had attributed this idea to Porphyry and called it a 'mere sophistry'. For him, what can happen between any two things is 'conjunction' (*ittiṣāl*), not unification (*ittiḥād*), because unification implies the transformation of two separate substances into one single being. It also means the destruction of the original entity and the emergence of a new one. By contrast, Ṣadrā posits the unification of the intellect and the intelligible as a condition for veritable knowledge because he considers the ultimate meaning of things to lie not in the things themselves, as the majority of the Peripatetics would assume, or in the mind, as most *kalām* thinkers would argue, but in the world of the disembodied intelligibles. The proper locus of knowledge is beyond the individual mind. Knowledge as articulated through human language emerges from an encounter between the knowing subject and the intelligible world. In short, knowledge is not a property of the knower.

This, in fact, is Ṣadrā's answer to one of the fundamental temptations of epistemology, namely the claim that we can encapsulate the full reality of existence in our mental constructions. Since existence is intrinsically self-intelligible and saturated with meaning, the knowing subject cannot claim to assign meaning to things. There is certainly an input coming from the human mind in all cognitive acts. Naming, for instance, is an essential component of all cognitive acts. We cannot know what we cannot name. To make something known is to give it a name and distinguish it from other beings. In this sense, there is no object of knowledge without the cognitive, conceptual and subjective input of the knowing subject.

Meaning in a wider sense of the term, however, cannot be grounded in the internal workings of the mind. For instance, when I know something about the oak tree in the garden, this knowledge comes about as a result of the encounter between my perceptual faculties such as seeing, sensing, etc., and the intelligible form of the tree. While I assign the names 'oak', 'tree' and 'garden' to actual objects in the outside world, they retain their ontological reality independent of me. It would be absurd to claim that things exist only when I know them. The mind turns to actually existing beings and 'intends' them in the phenomenological sense of the term. The fact that this is the knowledge *of* something outside and besides me refers to the non-subjective existence of things in the outside world. In Ṣadrā's words, 'perception is nothing more than the soul's attention to and witnessing of what is perceived' (*Asfār*, iii. 1. 162; 250–1).

This conceptual realism is further underlined by the fact that my ability to know is prompted by something outside my mind. Placed between the soul, which refers to the totality of my cognitive inventory, and the Active Intellect, which functions as the operative principle of knowledge, my mind responds to both the soul and the Active Intellect but also to what is beyond them: 'This capacity [to know things] is an intellective light, having an in-depth knowledge of existence and emanating on it from a principle which, to us, is a substance above the soul and below the Active Intellect'. This 'intellective light', a typical Ṣadrean expression, takes its reality from the self-illuminating nature of existence as it makes things visible by revealing their intellectual-cognitive form. Ṣadrā applies this principle to all acts of cognition to create meaning: the soul creates abstract meaning only in the sense of uncovering the intellective, formal meaning of things. We remain bounded to existence even at the highest level of abstraction. Ṣadrā derives both epistemic and moral lessons from this and says that 'the truth [of things] is larger and greater than to be encapsulated by a single mind; it is nobler and higher than to be made present by one single intellect or another' (*Mafātiḥ*, i. 80). Since our existence precedes our perception of things, we encounter reality in a framework of relations that is already saturated with meaning. From Ṣadrā's point of view, Descartes was wrong to deduce the certainty of my existence from my knowledge of myself. Instead of saying 'I think therefore I am', we should be saying 'I *am* therefore I think'.

Three types of knowledge

In his dense epistemological discussions, Ṣadrā works with three types of knowledge, each corresponding to a distinct ontological state. Empirical knowledge, employed by the scientist, gives us knowledge of things as matter, form, substance, accident, and so on. This type of knowledge corresponds to the corporeal reality of things and is indispensable for our physical understanding of the world. Logical and demonstrative method, used by philosophers and logicians, gives us knowledge of things as universals and general terms. This is qualitatively different from physical knowledge but equally necessary for a proper understanding of the reality of things because the human mind works with concepts. Without such general and abstract terms, we cannot perceive the world as a whole. Finally, realized or 'tasted' knowledge leads us to a direct vision of reality whereby we go beyond the material and the abstract and reach a degree of perception which enables us to see things as they are. This type of knowledge corresponds to a reality that transcends the corporeal and the mental. Its proper locus is the metaphysical and ontological reality of things, a level of reality from which things derive their existence as material, corporeal, abstract, mental or spiritual beings. Forms of cognition, whether empirical, logical or spiritual, are thus variations of the perception of the same reality, i.e., existence.

Since knowledge is the presence of something to itself and the absence of any barrier to seeing the thing itself, existence is the highest form of knowledge because existence is never absent from itself. This simple syllogism underlies an important aspect of Ṣadrā's being-centered epistemology: knowledge is neither a mental abstraction nor a property of the mind. Rather, knowledge is presence, light and clarity, because to know something is to 'see' and perceive its form, i.e., essential identity. Knowledge as clarity is a key component of medieval epistemology and goes back to the Greeks. Ṣadrā reworks this principle and argues that beings reveal themselves and make their intellective form 'present' to cognition in proportion to their state of existence. Since existence constantly 'presents' itself, knowing means perceiving this ever-dynamic 'presenting' (*ḥuḍūr*).

Existence lends itself to cognition and conceptualization to the extent to which it becomes a particular being. I know various aspects of existence through my senses and intellect. I can operate through these modalities to get an idea about existence. I can further make various connections between concepts and facts or between concepts and other concepts. But none of these gives me existence itself, i.e., existence-*qua*-existence. Since senses perceive things as particular beings and my mind knows them as abstract, general intelligibles, I cannot claim to know existence as it is. My epistemic tools to perceive the ordinary modalities of existence fall short of grasping and encapsulating existence as a whole.

Here Ṣadrā invites us to remember a key premise of his ontology: The difference between the *concept* and *reality* of existence has a direct bearing on how we know. As a concept, existence becomes an abstract notion, a universal that applies to a multitude of things. At this level of existence, which Ṣadrā calls 'mental existence', we operate through abstract and general concepts such as trees, animals, humans, etc. But the reality of things is different. What exists in the outside world is not 'tree', 'animal' or 'human' but an oak tree, a horse, a certain John, etc. The concept of existence as produced by the mind has an essential role to play in our cognitive encounter with the world. But it can never replace the reality of existence, which is always concrete, particular and non-repeatable.

Ways of knowing

The mind perceives things through general, abstract concepts. This is true for existence as well: what the mind perceives of existence is only its concept, not its reality. When transferred to the mind, the particular modalities of existence become 'mental existence'. This transformation moves us from first order experiences to second-order conceptualizations and puts a distance between reality and concept. Here is how Ṣadrā describes this 'distancing':

> Every concrete being represented in the mind with its reality ought to maintain its quiddity despite the change in its modality of existence. The reality of existence is such that it is in the extra-mental world. Everything whose reality is such that it is in the extra-mental world cannot be found in the mind [as it is] otherwise this would lead to the alteration of something from its own reality

[into something else]. Therefore the reality of existence cannot be found in any mind. What is represented of existence in the soul whereby it takes on universality and generality is not the reality of existence but one of the aspects of its constitution and one of its names. (*Asfār*, i. 1. 37–8)

The reality of existence, as distinct from its concept, does not allow generalities in the mental, abstract sense of the term. The general concepts and universals that we employ to define and describe existence as a concept apply not to existence itself but to its 'degrees of descent', i.e., particular modes. But even then we should be careful not to mistake the concept of existence for its reality and then draw fallacious conclusions. This explains Ṣadrā's frustration with the whole concept of 'representation' (*irtisām*) as the cornerstone of Avicennan epistemology and psychology. It is true that things leave certain 'impressions' on our minds. We see the mountain and develop an abstract image of it in our minds. The mental image of the mountain is obviously different from the actual mountain. The danger is to think that I can grasp the true meaning of the mountain through such mental images and impressions. What I know as the form of the mountain is not a mental concept or abstraction but its very reality. True, the physical mountain is not transplanted into my mind. But the 'form' of the mountain is no less real than the physical mountain. In fact, Ṣadrā's radical claim is that the former is absolutely more real than the latter because the fundamental reality of things is contained in their intelligible form, which is eventually united with their existence.

The main problem with the representational theory of knowledge, defended by the Peripatetics, is that it turns the reality of existence into a mental concept and then treats it as an abstract object to which various perceptual and cognitive properties are attributed a posteriori. Ṣadrā rejects the theory as a whole because 'the reality of existence cannot be obtained in the mind. What obtains in the mind concerning existence is only a mental consideration [i.e., concept], and it is one aspect [of existence] among its [other] aspects. The true knowledge of existence is based on witnessing and presence' (*Asfār*, i. 1. 61). Ṣadrā's critique of the representational theory of knowledge is thus based on his ultimate goal of reducing primary cognitive terms to existence and its self-grounding reality: 'knowledge is a kind of existence. As a matter of fact, knowledge and existence are one and the same thing' (*Asfār*, iii. 1. 150). Since knowledge is a mode of existence and obtained through direct witnessing, mere representation cannot capture its truth and identity.

All beings have consciousness

If knowledge is existence, then beings that partake of existence must have some degree of consciousness. This is true for all beings that exist regardless of their physical properties. The act of existing links beings to an intellective-cognitive principle beyond themselves. Ṣadrā insists on this point and adduces as evidence the etymology of the word *wujūd* and its derivations in Arabic. *Wujūd* comes from the radicals *w–j–d* and means 'finding'. The verb's fourth form *awjada* means 'to be found'. Existence implies a conscious act of finding and being found. Existence, meaning, intelligibility and consciousness are all essentially interrelated.

This unitary view of existence and meaning leads Ṣadrā to develop what I call 'ontological vitalism', i.e., the idea that all beings possess a degree of consciousness and intelligibility by virtue of the fact that they exist. Ṣadrā holds that 'whatever is established in existence is capable of being intelligible even potentially' (*Ittiḥād* in *Majmūʿa*, 71) but adds that 'the majority of intelligent people are incapable of understanding the penetration of knowledge, power, and volition in all things including stones and inanimate objects just like the penetration of existence in them' (*Asfār*, iii. 1. 335–6). The 'penetration of existence' in this particular context means that the entire cosmos is both alive and has consciousness. But each being's share in existence and consciousness is different and depends on the degree and intensity of its ontological constitution. In this sense, the more 'beingful' a thing is, the more life, reality, meaning and consciousness it possesses.

In a cosmological scheme, all beings yearn for their perfection and penultimate goal. Ṣadrā believes that 'all things are in love with God the Exalted, yearn to meet Him, and [... seek to reach] the abode of His munificence'. The 'ontological love' that penetrates the cosmos propels things to reach their natural perfection. Each being displays a different degree of love and yearning. But ultimately they all seek their final *telos* in their cosmological journey and this connects them to the rest of the universe: 'The hylé is completed through its form, the form through its forming agent, the sense through the soul, the soul through the intellect, and the intellect subsists through the Necessary Being' (*Asfār*, iii. 2. 150). What unites all these different degrees of existence is 'love', which underlies both the ontological foundation and cosmological journey of things. Ṣadrā puts this in evocative language:

> Love penetrates all beings because life penetrates all beings due to the penetration of existence in them. We have also stated before that existence as a single reality is the same as knowledge, power and life. An existing being cannot be conceived without the nature of existence in a general way. By the same token, an existing being cannot be thought of as having no knowledge and action, and whatever knows and does, regardless of how, has life.

In conclusion, according to the sages, everything is alive. But when the majority of people look at an animal, all they see is its external senses and its volitional movement from one place to another. (*Asfār*, iii. 2. 150)

In explicating his ontological vitalism, Ṣadrā follows the Qurʾānic descriptions of the world of nature in vitalistic terms. Various Qurʾānic verses refer to heavens, animals, the sun, the moon and the stars as praising God and prostrating before Him even though people do not understand their language. To quote Ṣadrā, 'existence in a general sense is identical with knowledge and consciousness in a general way. Because of this, the divine gnostics hold that all beings are cognizant of their Lord and prostrate before Him (*Asfār*, iv. 1. 164). Ṣadrā then adds: 'We argue that all animal, plant and inanimate natures have knowledge and consciousness by themselves, through the necessities of their essences, and their particular effects on account of their partaking of existence because existence is identical with light and manifestation. Existence is therefore united with the qualities of the perfection of existence in knowledge, power, volition, life, and the like' (*Kāshāniyya* in *Majmūʿa*, 137).

In these deliberations on the cognitive dimension of existence, Ṣadrā remains highly critical of the Peripatetics and Suhrawardī for holding that 'no corporeal being is alive by itself; every corporeal being in itself is dead and dark'. By contrast, he redefines life, consciousness and meaning as an effect of existence and links all beings, animate and inanimate alike, to one another through an ontological unity that forms the basis of both a vitalistic cosmology and non-subjectivist epistemology.

Self-knowledge and knowledge-by-presence

In his critique of the representational theory of knowledge, Ṣadrā does not completely rule out the possibility of such knowledge, but he does show its limits. The ontological spectrum of existence is such that there must be other types of knowledge corresponding to each level of existence. Knowledge of the self is a case in point. As Suhrawardī pointed out, self-knowledge cannot be an impression or representation of the self in the mind because there is no break between the self and its knowledge of itself. Knowledge of the self is identical with the self itself. When I say 'I am in pain' or 'I know myself', the subject and the predicate are one and the same. In such first-order propositions, the subject who says 'I am in pain' and the subject who is actually in pain are the same. In the case of second-order propositions, however, this unity is broken, and a distinction is introduced between the self and its judgment about itself. We know ourselves directly and without the intermediary of concepts or representations.

Since we are always 'present' to ourselves, our self-knowledge is secured through the kind of presence that underlies our self-awareness. This 'presential knowledge' is immediate and non-representational and confirms the unity of the knowing self and the object of knowledge. Suhrawardī, who was the first to give a clear formulation of knowledge-by-presence, gives the example of pain and says that when we are in pain, this fact is a direct, unmediated perception and cannot be the representation of pain in our minds. Otherwise, we would be talking about pain as an abstract notion rather than stating our actual pain. Interestingly enough, Wittgenstein uses the same example of pain to defend the thesis that *being in* pain is the same as having *consciousness of* pain.[1] This, again, confirms the unity of existence and knowledge.

But the example of pain applies to sense perception and sensate objects only. Since sensation is particular, subject to error, and cannot be a universal basis for veritable knowledge, knowledge-by-presence turns out to be very limited in scope. Ṣadrā does not accept this conclusion and parts ways with Suhrawardī. Instead, he seeks to establish knowledge-by-presence as the foundation of both sensate and conceptual knowledge. Since knowledge is a mode of existence and existence is always present and illuminating, true knowledge comes about through the presence of existence in our perceptual and intellective cognitions. The true knowledge of existence cannot be a representation; it must be based on presence and direct witnessing.

Our knowledge of ourselves is the same as our existence whereas the knowledge of our knowledge of ourselves is not our own existence but a mental form added to it. [This mental form] is not our personal identity, and has its own mental identity. By the same token, the knowledge that we have through this knowledge is a form added to the two former identities of knowledge, and this continues until mental consideration and representation come to an end... When we know our individual existential identity through an extraneous knowledge, this knowledge is only an accident that subsists through and is different from our existence, not comparable to ourselves. The same [principle] holds true for all knowledge about knowledge because all knowledge is a mode of existence and can be obtained not through another [mental] form but by itself. (*Asfār*, i. 3. 295–6)

This makes knowledge a real and non-abstract encounter with existence. To know is to participate in the intelligible reality of things and this participation cannot be a mental,

1 Wittgenstein, *Philosophical Investigations* (1968), §246.

abstract enterprise. The intelligible reality of things is more 'real' than their physical properties. We know something fully and veritably only when its intelligible form is present in our mind. This act of 'presenting' is not a solipsistic act because it involves the idea of my mind going out of itself and reaching out to the realm of intelligible substances. In this sense, all knowing is mediated by presential knowledge. 'Knowledge of self [obtained] through its faculties and specific effects such as its own self-knowledge takes place through presence (*ḥuḍūr*); but it may also take place through attainment (*ḥuṣūl*). Yet the former is necessary and continuous whereas the latter depends on appropriate time and conditions' (*Kāshāniyya* in *Majmūʿa*, 130). In conclusion, knowledge-by-presence precedes and underlies knowledge as representation and impression in an essential way.

Reason and revelation

In his philosophical, religious and mystical works, Ṣadrā works with several types of epistemology and tries to dovetail them in a way that would conform to the demands of both demonstrative reason and realized knowledge. In a discussion of God's knowledge of things, he says, referring to the views of the Sufis, that 'thus we have indeed made their unveiling, based on tasting, correspond to the principles of demonstration' (*Asfār*, iii. 1. 263). He considers 'religious law (*al-sharʿ*) combined with reason' as 'light upon light' (*Uṣūl*, i. 438). The relation between reason and revelation is not necessarily based on an antagonism because the truth is one and reveals itself in different forms. The truth of revelation and the truth of reason come from the same source. They clash when one seeks to supplant the other. Theology dries up when it rejects reason in the name of orthodoxy; philosophy exceeds its limits when it seeks to reduce reality to its own constructions. Ignorant ascetics turn themselves into 'fools' when they try to ban philosophy in the name of asceticism and spiritual experience (*Kasr*, 39).

In stating these bold points, Ṣadrā's working principle is that religion is more than 'faith' in the sense that most fideists use the term. Religion is more than just 'deeds' and thus goes beyond the realm of practical reason as Kant assumed it. Finally, religion is more than just 'feeling' as Schleiermeier and others have advocated. Religion entails all of these three but also a more fundamental dimension, i.e., the intellectual and cognitive content of faith and action. As Ṣadrā insists, the intellective principle that underlies existence and the cosmological order also underlies our human efforts to understand their meaning. The same applies to religion, revelation and the mission of the prophets. The 'niche of prophecy' is the fountainhead of philosophy because it guides human reason in the direction of universal principles. In this sense, the intellectual-cognitive dimension of faith and religion corresponds to the realm of pure reason but is no longer limited to the Kantian sense of the term because reason or intellect, as defined within the context of self-intelligible existence, already points to something beyond reason.

Revelation, intuition and reason complement each other and give us an integrated and holistic context for the meaning of the universe and our place in it. Their synthesis forms the basis of metaphysics – the only science that can overcome theological bickering and philosophical sophistry. According to Ṣadrā, God is the true founder of metaphysics: 'This science [of metaphysics] is too noble for it to have been able to be established by a human because God has established it through revelation and inspiration given to the prophets, peace be upon them, and the previous philosophers have taken the principles of this science from the niche of prophecy' (*Uṣūl*, i. 99). Revelation and prophecy are not substitutes for philosophy. Rather, they provide a context of meaning and intelligibility within which the human mind and heart function.

Ṣadrā extends this discussion to the relationship between philosophical and mystical knowledge. He agrees with Ibn Sīnā that there are two types of philosophers: those who 'engage in philosophy through tasting' (*ahl al-ḥikmat al-dhawqiyya*) and those who 'engage in philosophy through research' (*ahl al-ḥikmat al-baḥthiyya*).[1] Each has his own methods of enquiry and set of questions. A proper metaphysical vision combines both methods and perspectives and pays due attention to all levels of knowledge and cognition.

But what is the ultimate goal of knowledge? Ṣadrā's short, direct answer is to attain 'knowledge of God' (*maʿrifat Allāh*). It is the highest form of knowledge one can attain because it is the ultimate truth, bliss and salvation. In contrast to other types of knowledge which serve a purpose other than itself, the knowledge of God is sought for itself. It is through this knowledge and consciousness that we attain true happiness – the kind of happiness that completes our humanity. But reaching the knowledge of God and true happiness requires the cleansing of the heart so that 'God's majesty can be unveiled to it in His Essence, Qualities and Acts' (*Kasr*, 74). The heart, the primary locus of intellectual knowledge and spiritual perfection, must be clean to function like a mirror for the truth to shine upon.

Ṣadrā hastens to add that every deed, good or bad, has an effect on the state of the heart. 'Good states' come from

1 Ibn Sīnā, 'On the Rational Soul' in Dmitri Gutas, *Avicenna and the Aristotelian Tradition* (1988), 77–8.

good deeds just as immoral qualities come from evil deeds. Thus 'every good or bad deed, word, action or thought that emanates from the children of Adam has an effect on the states of his heart. God has referred to this in His verse: 'Whoever has done an atom of goodness shall see it and whoever has done an atom of evil shall see it' (*Zilzāl*, 99: 7–8)' (*Kasr*, 77–8). The import of this for action is clear: the goal is to attain a state of purity and goodness so that the truth can manifest itself in us. Heart-knowledge is our gateway to the Divine truth and gives us true happiness and repose.

HEART-KNOWLEDGE AND MORAL PERFECTION

This is underlined by another onto-epistemic principle: one's state of spiritual perfection is proportionate to one's proximity to the world of the intelligibilia. The closer we are to the intelligible reality of things, the more 'intellectual pleasure' and thus happiness we have. But this can happen only when we uphold the principle of detachment, i.e., detachment from the limitations and burdens of the material world as a condition of realized knowledge and happiness. As Ṣadrā states:

> Our self-consciousness is more intense when we leave the body because [at that moment] our presence to ourselves becomes more complete and firm. Since most people are immersed in their material bodies and occupied with them, they forget themselves. As God the Exalted said: 'They forgot God and God made them forget themselves' (*al-Ḥashr*, 59: 19). They do not perceive themselves because of this intense relationship except as mixed with their bodies. This is so because the conjunction of the soul with the body and its relation to it is like the conjunction of light with shadow, torch with smoke, and a person with his image in the mirror [...] When this relationship between the soul and the body is terminated and this obstacle disappears, the intelligibles become

visible, their consciousness present, their knowledge real (*ʿaynan*), and [their] perception an intellectual vision (*ruʾya ʿaqliyya*).

This leads to a view of existence, consciousness and happiness that makes detachment and disembodiment a condition of full realization:

Thus the pleasure of our intellective life becomes more perfect and nobler than all other forms of goodness and happiness. You have already learnt that real pleasure is existence and especially intellective existence due to its detachment from the mixture of non-existence. This is particularly true for the Real Beloved and the most perfect Necessary Being for it is the reality of existence that contains in itself all aspects of existence. Partaking of Its pleasure is the highest pleasure and repose. In fact, it is the repose in which there is no worry. (*Asfār*, iv. 2. 124–5)

We can never reach full repose and happiness as long as we live in this world because we remain conditioned by its material limitations. We can, however, overcome it through 'death' to the world, as stated in the famous hadith of the Prophet of Islam: 'Die before you die.' For Ṣadrā, this death towards the temptations of the world is the standing condition of a spiritual rebirth, which is also a way of participating in the intelligible world:

Know that existence is goodness and happiness, and the consciousness of existence is also goodness and happiness. But existents are of varying degrees in terms of perfection and imperfection. Whenever existence is more perfect, its detachment from non-existence is more [real], and happiness in it is more immediate. And whenever it is imperfect, its mixture with evil and misfortune is more. Now, the most perfect and noble of all existents is the First Truth, which is worthy of [comprehension] first by the separate intellective existents and then by the souls. The lowest of existents is prime matter, time, and motion, and then material forms, then natural forms, and then souls....

Since existents are of different degrees, happiness, which is their perception, also allows different degrees of superiority. The existence of intellective faculties is thus superior to the existence of animal faculties of desire and anger... When our souls become stronger, terminate their relations with the body, and return to their true identity and source, they acquire a joy and happiness incomparable to sensual pleasures. This is so since the cause of this pleasure [i.e., the consciousness of existence] is the strongest, most complete and immediate of all joyous pleasures. (*Asfār*, iv. 2. 121–2)

The heart is the proper locus of the knowledge of existence based on direct witnessing, existential encounter and unveiling. Since the meaning of existence can be grasped through 'unveiling' and 'illuminative presence', the only faculty capable of this function is the 'spiritual heart'. As an epistemic-spiritual faculty, the heart arrives at a synthesis for all the different faculties within the human person and comes closest to perceiving the reality of things as they are: 'The noblest part in the human being is the real heart, and it is something indivisible and reaches completion and perfection only through knowledge and gnosis. And there is no doubt that the noblest of all knowledge is the knowledge of God' (*Kasr*, 33).

By assigning to the heart a major epistemic function, Ṣadrā underscores the importance of Qurʾānic references to the heart as a source and faculty of knowledge (e.g., *al-Aʿrāf*, 7: 179: 'They have hearts but do not understand with them; they have eyes but do not see with them'. See also *al-Ḥajj*, 22: 46, *Muḥammad*, 47: 24.) The heart is where the intellectual spiritual reality of things is most visibly manifested. Heart-knowledge is thus this universal knowledge that unites man's horizon with the horizon of existence. Furthermore, it leads to the unity of intellectual truth and spiritual-moral perfection. Since knowledge is existence, there is no true knowledge without it transforming our existence.

The four degrees of perfection which Ṣadrā mentions below underlie the unity of conceptual and moral-spiritual perfection:

There are four degrees of perfection [in knowing things]: the first is the refinement of one's outward state (*al-ẓāhir*) by following Divine orders and Prophetic law. The second is the refinement of one's inward state (*al-bāṭin*) and cleaning the heart from dark and despicable habits and behaviour. The third is the illumination [of the soul] by the forms of knowledge and favourable qualities. The fourth is the [spiritual] extinction of the soul from itself and fixing its gaze upon contemplating the First Lord and His Magnificence.

This is the end of journeying towards God by following the path of the soul. After these stages, there are still many stations and degrees, which are not less than what one has followed before. But one should prefer to shorten [the discussion of] what one does not perceive except through witnessing and presence. This is due to the inability to explain what one does not comprehend except through light. As for those who have attained spiritual perfection, after they have journeyed to God and reached Him, there are other journeys [for them], some of which are in the Truth and some of which are from the Truth but with the Truth. (*Shawāhid*, 207–8)

The soul and spiritual anthropology

Following the tradition, Ṣadrā defines the 'soul' (*nafs*) as an ability or 'potency' (*quwwa*) to carry out certain acts. In the philosophical jargon of traditional philosophy, this is 'a form of perfection' whereby a living being receives and produces certain 'effects'. In broad outline, this corresponds to Aristotle's first or primary 'entelechy', i.e., the capacity of an animate being to reach perfection in its species. These effects and acts constitute perfection for animate beings because they make them perfect or 'complete' in their species and establish them as beings with an actual impact on the world. Like the Greek and Muslim Platonists, Ṣadrā held that a being is more perfect when it is actual. Actuality is a mode of perfection by which the world is sustained.

The soul designates a being's ability to bring about effects in the world such as moving, feeding, perceiving, responding, etc. 'We call a soul every active potency from which effects [in the world] emanate according to more than one fashion [i.e., with multiple effects]' (*Asfār*, iv. 1. 6). In this basic sense, the soul is not a thing or being but capacity, a potency to take on multiple tasks in the external world. This definition of the soul, however, is already based on a concept of life or 'animation' because the soul applies only to those beings that perform 'acts of life such as sensation and voluntary motion'. A tree has a 'soul' because it is alive but fire or earth does not because they cannot produce the effects of living beings.

The soul as the perfection of the body

Like al-Fārābī and Ibn Sīnā, Ṣadrā concurs that the soul can be defined as potency, form or perfection. But it is more correct to define it as perfection because the form is inscribed in matter whereas the soul remains above and detached from the body. Strictly speaking, the soul is not the form but the perfection of the body because it enables the body to be what it is. This gives us the fundamental meaning of perfection in natural philosophy: perfection is the fulfillment of the necessary conditions of a species. The soul as perfection for the animal makes it a proper member of its species. The same applies to plants and other living beings. To belong to the animal species means having the necessary qualities of being an animal, i.e., motion and sensation. The soul gives these fundamental qualities to the animal and thus perfects it in its species (*Asfār*, iv. 23). Furthermore, the perfection which the soul brings to its agent is gradational. For corporeal beings, perfection is not an end-state but a process. The soul is accordingly not a static but a dynamic being engaged in a continuous journey to reach its perfection. This is well captured in the rich etymology of the word *nafs* in Arabic, which, among other things, is related to 'breath', referring to the dynamic ebb and flow of being alive.

Does the soul consist of only the functions it performs? If one takes a non-substantive, performative view of the soul, the soul appears to be reducible to its functions. It is like the mind which is nothing but the thoughts it possesses. But this would be considering the soul only from the point of view of the functions it performs rather than the 'substance' (*jawhar*) that it is. The soul performs the actions it does through its essential properties. This suggests that the soul must have some sort of an existence independent of its primary functions. Furthermore, the soul has a unity, which is reflected in the various tasks it performs without losing its essential identity. In fact, this is one of the traditional proofs for the existence of the soul: while human beings change in their bodily form, they retain their identity. The soul signifies this identity. This is where we go beyond the soul as a corporeal entity and begin to look for 'a type of science other than physics' (*Asfār*, iv. 1. 10).

The 'soulness of the soul' or the soul-qua-soul has a unique type of being. Even though its primary purpose is to perform certain functions such as motion and perception, its relation to these functions is not like the relation of a father to fatherhood or a writer to authorship. The relation of a father to fatherhood is an accidental relationship and does not define the essence of the human person. We can make a clear distinction between the essential and accidental properties of a being and describe their different functions without confusing them.

Soul and body

But the soul's relationship to the body is not like this. As the potency, form and perfection of the body, the soul has a substantive relationship to the body. It is a relationship of unison rather than functionality. The soul commands dominion over the body as an organic whole, not like a superior yet eventually accidental agent. The way the soul acts upon the body is different from the way a captain sails his ship or a mason builds a house. The captain's existence is external and accidental to the ship just as is the mason's existence to the building. But the soul acts upon and operates through the body in an essential, unitary way. 'The soul's attachment to and dominion over the body is a matter of essence and takes place through its own particular existence' (*Asfār*, iv. 1. 12). Furthermore, the soul exercises power over all of the organs and faculties of the body, from the vegetative and animal to the spiritual potencies. It is the soul that causes the various acts and effects through its penetration of the body. By the same token, it is not the sense organs but the soul that perceives the particular forms that obtain in the senses. The soul, a spiritual substance in essence, uses the five senses as its instruments. The five senses, having no independent reality on their own, are like the 'soldiers of the heart, i.e., the rational soul' (*Asfār*, iv. 1. 137). This is a reference to the

Qur'ānic verses 'No one knows the soldiers of your Lord save He' (*al-Mudaththir*, 74: 31).

But how does the soul, which is a spiritual being, perceive particular, material substances? This can be seen as part of a larger question in metaphysics: how do the spiritual and the bodily meet each other? This is one of the key problems in epistemology and also points to the mind–body problem. As it should be clear by now, Ṣadrā does not work within a dualist framework – a framework that has shaped Western philosophical and psychological thinking since at least Descartes. There is no such thing as mind or soul on the one hand and body on the other, cut off from each other and waiting to be connected. Rather, since existence is one, all of its reflections, sub-categories and particularizations are interconnected, leaving no room for radical ruptures in existence and its particular modes. As Ṣadrā never tires of reminding us, existence is graded and lends itself to multiple layers and stratifications without a break or disconnect in substantial attributes. 'Existence is a circle turning around itself' creating its own apogee as well as the lowest point in its self-delimitation. When it descends into lower forms, it takes on particular, material and corporeal attributes and becomes a mineral or plant. When it ascends into higher forms of reality, it displays fuller forms of being and becomes an intellective substance or an angelic being. There is no rupture in existence but only gradation.

The unity of the soul

It is against this ontological background that Ṣadrā explains the unity of the human soul. While we humans have multiple faculties and qualities, we always see ourselves as one. We possess such contradictory tendencies as love and hatred, knowledge and ignorance, mercy and wrath. We also have bodily organs which have limited capabilities. In addition to these, we have our soul, our main substance as a rational being. Furthermore, we are born, grow up, get old and go through various stages of life. In the end, though, we have one soul, one consciousness, one self, one rational substance. This is so because the soul is one and indivisible. And what secures this unity is the rational soul.

As a unitary substance, 'the human soul by itself perceives the universals and the particulars'. The way it perceives these substances without losing its unity is ultimately a mystery but Ṣadrā's gradational ontology provides some clues. Clearly, the soul does not relate to the physical world in a mechanical way. It is more like a process of penetration, effusion and conjunction. To better describe this, Ṣadrā makes a startling comparison and refers to the way the four Archangels interact with the world: they are the primary soldiers of God on earth for performing His commands. They penetrate the world without becoming contained in it.

The soul, which is 'a substance from the Lord and a secret of the Exalted', works in a similar way. It perceives and acts upon the world of universals and particulars without losing its essential identity. It penetrates the world without being dissolved by it. When the soul interacts with the world of creation, it gains something and becomes more perfect spiritually because 'the world of creation is a path to the Truth' (*Asfār*, iv. 1. 129). But its proper abode is not the material world, which can imprison it. It is a spiritual being destined to attain a higher degree of realization. Thus when the rational human person 'perfects his intellect with knowledge and cleans his intellect through disengagement from corporeal bodies, he becomes one of God's angels in actuality' (*Asfār*, iv. 1. 137).

What we have here is a two-fold view of the soul. On the one hand, the soul is a collection of functions and effects executed through the body. As far as its performative nature is concerned, the soul belongs to the realm of the corporeal and is studied under physics. On the other hand, however, the soul is a spiritual substance whose essence goes beyond the corporeal-physical realm. Its perfection lies in its non-material capacity to act on the body. This dual nature of the soul complements Ṣadrā's dynamic view of the cosmos and substantial motion. As we discussed before, Ṣadrā's natural philosophy is based on a fluid and integrative understanding of the physical order of things. Existence is self-generating and gradational and thus breaks down the rigid categories of matter and form, corporeal and spiritual, vegetative and animal, animal and human, and so on. Ṣadrā's definition of the soul as 'corporeal in origination, spiritual in subsistence' integrates well into his ontology and cosmology. This is how Ṣadrā describes the corporeal origination and spiritual subsistence of the soul:

The human soul has many levels and stations, from the beginning of its generation to the end of its goal; and it has certain essential states and modes of being. At first, in its state of connection (with the body) it is a corporeal substance. Then it gradually becomes more and more intensified and develops through the different stages of its natural constitution until it subsists by itself and moves from this world to the other world, and 'so returns to its Lord' (*al-Fajr,* 89: 27).

Thus the soul is originated in a corporeal (state), but endures in a spiritual (state). The first thing to be generated in its states (of connection with the body) is a corporeal power; next is a natural form; then the sensible form with its levels; then the cogitative and the recollective; and then the rational soul. Next, after the practical intellect, it acquires the theoretical intellect according to its various degrees, from the rank of the intellect in potency to that of the intellect in actuality and the Active Intellect – which is the same as that 'Spirit' of the divine Command which is ascribed to God in His saying: *Say: 'The Spirit is from my Lord's Command!'* (*al-Isrā*, 17: 85).[1]

As a physical-cum-spiritual being, the human person has the capacity to move both upward and downward. He can confine himself to the corporeal or dwell in the spiritual. The soul lends itself to both possibilities. What elevates the soul from the corporeal to the spiritual is intelligence and will, the ability to distinguish between good and evil, and acting accordingly. The celebrated dictum 'whoever knows his soul/self knows his Lord' refers to this integral view of the human person. Coming to know oneself means recognizing one's physical qualities as well as spiritual potentialities. But more importantly, this knowledge is key to knowing God who grants perfection to all beings. Self-knowledge is a mode of spiritual perfection that enables us to see our humanity within the larger context of meaning and value that pours forth from the infinite mercy of God.

The human state and the perfect man

Traditional philosophers thought about the human being within such a larger context of meaning and intelligibility. Man, while displaying both noble and base qualities, was never considered to be a self-sufficient being. His existence, intelligence, emotions and other qualities made sense only within a matrix of non-subjectivist existential properties and cosmological relations. The human person occupies a special

1 Ṣadrā, *The Wisdom of the Throne* (*al-Ḥikmat al-ʿarshiyya*) (1981), 131–2.

place in the great chain of being to the extent to which he realizes his moral and spiritual potentials. When Mullā Ṣadrā speaks about the human state as the 'perfect man', he does not envision any kind of humanism in the ancient Greek or modern senses of the term. 'Humanism' as a philosophy of human subjectivism does not emerge as a possibility for Ṣadrā. Protagoras' motto 'man is the measure of all things' earned him, in Plato's eyes, the highest place among the Sophists but failed to explain how such a feeble being as the human could be accorded a special place among beings. Man with his human qualities has a higher ontological status than other beings because he has 'a share of the divine attributes' (*Protagoras*, 322) making him part of a reality larger than himself.

A proper analysis of the human state must therefore take into account three levels of reality: the human, the universe, and the Divine. The generic term for the human in Arabic, *al-insān*, refers to both the human person and the state in which the founding qualities of humanity are gathered. That is why Ibn ʿArabī, Ṣadrā's most important source on this issue, describes the 'perfect man' not only as a particular human being but also as a state of existence in which God's names and attributes are manifested in their totality. This is the stage where the absolutely one God begins to create and allows other beings to exist besides Himself. The universe exists in an orderly fashion because it is sustained by the Supreme Artisan. But the meaning of physical-external existence is completed only when it is connected to the higher meanings given to the perfect man. God has taught the perfect man all the names and made him His vicegerent on earth. He has made all beings in the world subservient to him and asked His angels to bow before him. With these exceptional gifts, man has been made to carry the burden of unity and justice on earth for all creation. In that sense, the perfect man is also the 'first intellect' representing the storehouse of all knowledge in a summary fashion.

While the universe displays a unity and harmony, it is the human state that brings it to completion because its meaning is fully realized when the human element is inserted into it. Ṣadrā says that

> the human is the last being by which the world of nature has been finalized. It is in the human state that the truths of the low and high universe have been combined. It is the human that has added the truths of the universe to the truths of the True One's Names and Qualities by which man's great caliphate in the big universe has obtained after his minor caliphate in the world of nature. (*Asfār*, ii. 2. 350)

The human state, while always susceptible to corruption and deviation, represents the highest form of God's creation because God has taught 'all the names' only to Adam who is endowed with the same intelligence that underlies the essential structure of things. The 'perfect man' (*al-insān al-kāmil*) completes the world of creation because it is through him that God's mercy is most fully displayed. Only the perfect human state can reveal the infinite truth and beauty of God's wisdom and generosity.

THE AESTHETICS OF EXISTENCE AND THE BEAUTY OF THE FORM

In his existential-spiritual journey, the human person encounters the universe as an order of being with harmony, beauty and proportion. As we have discussed, these qualities are intrinsic and real and can be experienced by the intelligent human person. This leads us to what we might call an 'aesthetics of existence', an aesthetics that appreciates the universe for both its substance and form. The universe is essentially beautiful because it reflects the infinite beauty of its Creator. It is only accidentally ugly.

It has been reported that God is beautiful and He loves beauty. He is the artisan of the universe and brings it into existence in His form, as He says, *[Say:] 'Everyone acts according to their form'* [*al-Isrā*, 17: 84]. And your forgiving Lord is merciful. So the entire universe is of the utmost beauty because it is a mirror for the Real. This is why the knowers have become enraptured by it and the verifiers have realized [their goal] through its love. For He is the object of gaze in every eye, the beloved in every form of love, the object of worship in every act of worship, and the [ultimate] goal in both the unseen and the seen. The entire universe prays to Him, praises Him, and glorifies Him. (*Tafsīr*, i. 153–4)

For Ṣadrā, beauty is as an ontological quality and has its own objective existence. It is ingrained in the nature of things. Just like the degrees of existence and knowledge, beauty also comes in different degrees, and human beings have different capacities to recognize it in its various manifestations. While the spiritual wayfarer looks for the inner beauty of things, this does not preclude him from pursuing outward beauty and work on his external beauty. Thus Ṣadrā says that,

as for beauty, its benefit in the world is clear. Ugly natures are detested [by everyone], and the necessities that are beautiful are closer to being provided and have a larger place in one's chest [consciousness]. Every spring of water in this world is also a spring in the hereafter. This is why the beauty that you see in most people is a proof for the nobility of the soul. When the light of the soul completes its illumination, it manifests itself in the body. What is looked at and what is known [of a person] often complement each other. Therefore the people of perspicacity, in their knowledge of the perfection of the soul, have provided for the external constitution of the body. To that effect, they have said that the face and the eye are a mirror for what is inside. (*Tafsīr*, i. 129)

Just as the universe displays both an inward and outward beauty, so do human beings. This is also reflected in their relations and dealings with other human beings. Taking note of this subtle point, Ṣadrā relates a saying attributed to the Prophet of Islam: 'Ask for what is best in regard to the beauty of faces'. He also refers to a juridical rule concerning the prayers with the community: when everybody is equal in their qualification to lead the prayer, the one with the most beautiful face should be the Imam.

THE PROBLEM OF EVIL AND THE BEST OF ALL POSSIBLE WORLDS

As an intrinsic aspect of the world of existence, beauty is related to goodness. By contrast, ugliness is related to evil. But why is there evil in the world? Why did an infinitely good and merciful God create a universe in which there is evil? We are confronted with the conundrum of theodicy here. If we say that God was able to create a world free of all evil but did not, then this goes against His infinite goodness. If we say that He was unable to stop evil from entering into the order of existence, then this puts severe limitations on His power.

Like their Jewish and Christian counterparts, this problem of theodicy has occupied the minds of Muslim thinkers over the centuries. Ṣadrā has discussed the issue in some detail. His main arguments can be summarized in this way:

The existence of evil in the universe is real. Both natural evil such as natural disasters and poisonous animals and moral evil perpetrated by free-willing human beings are part and parcel of the world-order in which we live. But evil is not an absolute in itself. Rather, it is the privation of goodness and arises when goodness is absent for either natural or moral reasons. Sickness, for instance, is the absence of health, blindness the absence of sight, falsehood the absence of truth, injustice the absence of justice, and so on.

Here Ṣadrā posits goodness as the fundamental cosmic principle and adds that 'goodness is that which everything desires, to which everything is inclined, and with which their goal of attaining whatever perfection is possible within their reach is achieved' (*Asfār*, iii. 2. 58). Since pure evil must go back to absolute non-being and absolute non-being cannot exist, all evil is relative as the privation of things vis-à-vis God's absolute being. When we look at 'all the things in this world which the majority of people call evil, we do not find them as evil in themselves but only by accident' (*Asfār*, iii. 2. 62).

The same principle applies to moral evil. Such moral evils as robbery, injustice, wrongful killing and fornication are evil only in relation to the moral requirement that they should be avoided. In Ṣadrā's words, they are evil when committed against 'reason and religion' (*Asfār*, iii. 2. 105). There are two main reasons why these acts in and of themselves are not evil. First of all, they serve other purposes for the material welfare of human beings. In the case of fornication, which is forbidden by both reason and religion, for instance, what is evil is not the source of fornication, i.e., the desire itself because 'desire is a praised quality in itself insofar as its reality, which is love, is concerned' and also because of its role 'in determining masculine and feminine forms and its being the reason for the preservation of the [human] species and procreation'. Fornication becomes evil when desire stops listening to reason. The second and probably more important reason is that 'all acts of obedience and disobedience... are matters of existence, and existence cannot be devoid of (some) goodness in one way or another' (*Asfār*, iii. 2. 104).

This admittedly optimistic view of moral evil can be seen as an extension of Ṣadrā's concept of existence as the primary source of goodness:

The condemned moral characters that prevent human souls from reaching their intellective perfection – like avarice, cowardice, wastefulness, pride, and vanity, and such wicked acts as injustice, wrongful killing, adultery, theft, calumny, defamation, obscenity, and the like – are not evil in themselves but rather states of goodness emanating from existence. They are [states of] perfections for natural entities and animal or vegetative powers that we find in man. Their evilness is only in comparison to a higher and nobler power which, in its perfection, has command over the disobedient and non-compliant powers under it. (*Asfār*, iii. 2. 61)

This is further underlined by the essential goodness of what is actual and the evilness of what is potential, i.e., weak existence:

Goodness in things comes from the fact that they are actual whereas evil stems from what is potential. A thing cannot be evil in every respect otherwise it would be non-existent. And no being, insofar as it is something existent, is evil. It becomes evil as a privation of perfection such as ignorance, or it necessitates its own non-existence in other things such as injustice.

Since potentiality has some sort of actualization in the external world, its essence subsists by existence. And existence... is prior to essence in an absolute way. Therefore, potentiality as potentiality has external realization only in the mind. It is then concluded that the actual is prior to the potential in terms of causation, nature, perfection, time and actual reality. (*Asfār*, iii. 2. 57–8)

The privative view of evil thus considers evil an accidental and temporal absence of goodness. In this sense, the universe is essentially good and no amount of natural and moral evil can alter its nature. Furthermore, evil is a contrastive and necessary component of a larger good built into the present world-order. What appears to be evil in relation to a particular immoral or harmful effect is no longer seen as evil in itself. In both cases, evil is relativized. The moral history of humanity is underlined by the presence of evil and ugliness as a test for human beings' moral choices: 'The reason why the human souls are found in this world [in which there is evil and suffering] is the testing of the children of Adam with these worldly misfortunes that have surrounded them because of sin and disobedience. This was in fact the single mistake their father Adam and mother Eve committed 'when they tasted of the [forbidden] tree' and 'became conscious of their nakedness' (*al-Aʿrāf*, 7: 22)' (*Tafsīr*, v. 270).

These moral considerations are further supported by Ṣadrā's ontology whereby he defends the famous thesis that, to use Ghazālī's phrase, 'there is nothing in the world of possibility more perfect and wonderful than what already is' (*laysa fī l-imkān abdaʿ mim-mā kān*). This is the celebrated doctrine of the 'best of all possible worlds' according to which 'the world-order as it is is the noblest, most perfect and highest of all the possible orders in that no other order can be conceived as higher than it'. Since God acts optimally and creates everything for a reason, the present world-order which He created is also the most optimal mode of creation and has a specific purpose for its existence. Moreover, God acts with wisdom and mercy intending the ultimate goodness of His creation: 'The Divine Providence requires that nothing be neglected but rather that everything reach its perfection'

(*Asfār*, iii. 2. 59). Since the goal of God's actions is 'universal welfare and goodness' (*Asfār*, iii. 2. 99), the individual cases of evil, imperfection, injustice and the like cannot overrule the overall goodness of things.

There are also ontological necessities for the existence of what appears to be evil and imperfection. Ṣadra's thesis is that the world cannot take pure goodness without ceasing to exist. The world is by definition something less than God, and this makes it radically imperfect and incomplete. Such an order of reality cannot sustain the intensity of pure goodness and pure light: 'If all of the lower beings were full of light, the matter of the cosmos would be destroyed by the burning of the light of the higher [beings]' (*Asfār*, iii. 2. 122). We cannot expect the world to be what it is and then demand it to be free of all evil and imperfection.

The universe is based on remarkable balance, harmony and proportion. But this harmony is also a result of the interplay of opposites: 'The interaction of opposite qualities that takes place in this world is the reason for the continuation of the effusion [of life]. This is goodness in relation to the universal world-order and evil in relation to particular individuals' (*Asfār*, iii. 2. 71). Furthermore, 'without contradiction there would be no generation and corruption, and without generation and corruption there would be no infinite number of individuals... the interaction between the opposites is a necessity so that there would be balance' (*Asfār*, iii. 2. 77). In conclusion, this is the best of all possible worlds from the points of view of God Himself, the moral test of human beings, and the ontological necessity of the universe. This is how Ṣadrā rounds off his argument:

This [i.e., what we have said so far] is only an example of the subtleties of God's providence and generosity for His creatures that are manifest. No one can covet the knowledge of the subtleties and mysteries of [God's] generosity and mercy in His invisible world and exalted angelic domain. Nor can one enumerate the beauties of creation and wisdom in beings, which make us supple in long lives since the knowledge of scholars is slight and inconsiderable in comparison to what the prophets and saints, peace be upon them, know. What they know is still very little in comparison to the knowledge of the angels who are in God's proximity and those human beings who are close to God through their standing presence before Him.

Now, even if we add all the knowledge of the angels, the jinn and the humans to God's knowledge, this would not qualify to be called 'knowledge'. It should be called puzzlement, wonder, incapacity, and imperfection rather than knowledge and wisdom. The real wisdom is the knowledge of things as they are. As it was mentioned before, the knowledge of a thing in its essence is a mode of its existence, and nothing encompasses things except their source and giver of existence. Thus there is no real knower/sage except God alone. The attribution of wisdom and knowledge to others is only a metaphor and parable. That is why it has been addressed to all beings through His words that 'of knowledge you have been given but little' (*al-Isrā*, 17: 85). (*Asfār*, iii. 2. 147–8)

ESCHATOLOGY: THE RETURN AND THE RESURRECTION

Ṣadra's eschatology is an extension of his ontology and cosmology as applied to the problem of resurrection and the hereafter. His main deliberations on existence and substantial motion apply to the 'beginning and end' of things, and the 'end' in question means a return to the starting point of all things. The great chain of being holds everything together from the creation and preservation of created beings to their return to their origin. What happens in between defines the nature and shape of our 'return', i.e., our resurrection in the afterlife. The cognitive and moral state of our existence in this journey determines the physical and spiritual conditions of our resurrection. Eschatology is both an onto-cosmological and a moral process.

For Ṣadra, the question of resurrection, the state of the soul in the graveyard, at the reckoning, the gathering, the opening of the book of deeds, the setting up of the scale and other issues are among the pillars of faith and principles of wisdom. A proper discussion of the question requires the unity of religious faith and philosophical analysis. Many have faltered in this because they have not taken 'the lights of wisdom from the niche of this final Prophet, peace and blessings be upon Him' (*Asfār*, iv. 2. 179). In keeping with the religious and philosophical tradition, Ṣadrā reiterates the belief in resurrection and the afterlife. The naturalists deny the resurrection of the body because they consider the human to comprise of the fleshly body which, when it disintegrates, cannot be resuscitated. In fact, Galen had his own doubts about this. Most theologians in the Islamic period consider bodily resurrection only and base their explanations on the physical descriptions of heaven and hell in the Qurʾān. The philosophers concentrate on intellectual and spiritual resurrection and neglect bodily resurrection, probably under the influence of the naturalists. The Qurʾān is firm on the afterlife and provides vivid details of heaven and hell, both promising and warning the mortal humans. The question is not so much whether there will be an afterlife but rather what kind of a life it will be and how the human resurrection will take place. Since the Qurʾān describes the afterlife in both spiritual and physical terms, Muslim scholars have proposed different explanations for spiritual and physical resurrection. Ṣadrā criticizes theologians and philosophers for providing an incomplete and contradictory exposition of the resurrection and afterlife.

Ṣadrā deploys his concept of existence to deduce that all beings will be re-created and realize their ultimate goal in the hereafter. As we have discussed before, it is existence rather than essence that is the foundational principle of things. Existence lends itself to gradation and takes on multiple forms and degrees of intensity. Likewise, it is 'form' rather than matter that defines the essence of things. Applied to the human person, this suggests that the soul rather than the body represents and holds together the human state. The preservation of the body is dependent upon the soul, not vice versa. The same holds true in the hereafter with the important difference that the body that will be resurrected will be of a different kind:

> The truth of resurrection goes back to the revival of the dead and the extraction of forms from matter, and the extraction of the souls from the bodies with a different kind of existence, and the replacement of their existence with an existence that is higher, more luminous and more knowing. In fact, ignorance is death greater [than physical death] and knowledge is life nobler [than life in this world]. (*Asfār* iv. 2. 176)

The Old and New Testaments of the Bible and the Qur'ān appear to contradict each other in regard to the details of resurrection and afterlife but eventually agree on the main points. A similar contradiction exists in regards to the views of the later philosophers. Ṣadrā believes that these seeming contradictions can be overcome but one needs a proper ontology to do so. To that effect, he outlines his view of physical and spiritual resurrection in 11 points, which can be summarized as follows (*Asfār*, iv. 2. 185–97):

Existence is the principal reality. The true identity of a being is its existence, not its essence. The particularization and individuation of a being depends on its existence. What we call 'accidents' are only constitutive and necessary elements of a being, not its true reality. Existence is graded and thus lends itself to intensification and diminution, perfection and imperfection, priority and posteriority, and so on. Graded existence is subject to change at all times. The 'movement of intensification' characterizes the existential journey of particular beings. Beings move towards greater perfection. The form, not the matter of a being constitutes its reality. A sword is what it is because of its form, i.e., the essence which gives it meaning and definition rather than its metal, colour, etc. The form or essence of things is separate from and above their material accidents. By the same token, man's essential nature is above his body. The destruction of the body at the moment of death does not lead to the disappearance of the human person; the 'person' takes on a different and a higher mode of existence.

The unity of beings is secured by their existence. Existence and unity are identical. Corporeal beings cannot have contradictory qualities at the same time. Black and white cannot be found in the same object simultaneously. But the human essence, by virtue of its existential intensification and higher ontological status, can overcome contradictory qualities and contain multiple meanings in it. The human person is one and unitary when perceiving multiple sensible objects. In this sense, there is no contradiction for the human person to be related to matter, i.e., body on the one hand, and to the spirit on the other. The human essence is related to the body but can overcome it. In fact, human beings can move up in the ladder of existence to reach the purely intelligible world of the Divine. Human identity is one and united through its stages of substantial motion, sensate change, etc.

The faculty of imagination, which connects the sensate to the spiritual, is not located in any part of the human body. It belongs to the world of detached substances and acts as an intermediary between the two worlds of detached intelligible substances and material, natural beings. Imaginal forms coexist with the human soul. The soul needs the bodily form to sense things. But this need becomes less as it moves up in existential intensification. This is a move from sensate existence to the imaginal forms and then to the purely intelligible. At higher levels of existence, the soul does not need sensate and corporeal forms. The form or essence of things does not need matter when it intensifies. It,s mode of existence becomes more intense. At this level, matter ceases to be a standing condition of existence. Imaginal forms thus become more real and effectual than physical, sensate objects. This suggests that the separation of the soul from the body does not diminish the reality and identity of the soul; to the contrary, it makes it more real. In this sense, the soul becomes more real after death and takes on an existentially stronger essence in the afterlife.

The soul stands in relation to three worlds: physical-natural, sensate-perceptual, and intelligible-archetypal. These three levels of existence have their own qualities, and beings relate to them in proportion to their state of existence. But the human person is related to all three at the same time. His identity is such that it starts out in the physical, moves to the sensible, and then to the purely intelligible and the spiritual. Ṣadrā calls them 'second man' and 'third man' respectively. Throughout this journey, the human person preserves his essence and identity but becomes less or more of an intelligible and spiritual being depending on his existential and moral state. The human person thus begins with a 'material existence' and continues with an 'otherworldly existence'.

In conclusion, humans will be resurrected in the next world with both body and spirit but the mode of their existence will be different. The ultimate destiny of our 'otherworldly existence' will be determined by our state of existence at the moment of death. Those who have reached the truth will be the happy ones and thus have a subtle body, possessing many meanings, intelligible forms and pleasures of an otherworldly nature. The human person who starts his earthly journey as a bodily, corporeal substance thus ends up as an intelligible, spiritual being spanning the entire gamut of existence and its multiple levels. When he completes his journey, he becomes a more perfect, fully realized and more 'beingful' substance, ready to reunite with the Origin, Beginning and Principle of his existence.

5

Conclusion: throwing away the ladder of philosophy

In one of his scant remarks on social philosophy, Ṣadrā reiterates the traditional definition of man as social animal and stresses that no single human being can manage to live like a human being by himself alone. Wild nature is beautiful but not enough for survival; the raw food there can be beneficial but cannot sustain human life without compromise. One needs others for the ultimate goal of living a 'good life' which is possible, according to Aristotle, with 'wisdom', i.e., making sense of the world through reason and virtue, and acting accordingly. Humans have been endowed with many remarkable qualities such as seeing, walking, doing, making, thinking, talking, etc. These qualities make life more meaningful, bring humans closer to one another, and help them build a civilized habitat. They are essential for the meaning of being human.

The most precious of them, however, is man's ability to reach the higher states of existence by appropriating 'universal meanings': 'Among the most special qualities that are reserved for the human person is the perception of universal meanings that are fully disengaged from matter... What is even more special than all of these is the conjunction of some human souls with the Divine realm whereby they become annihilated from themselves and subsist with Its subsistence. This is when the Truth becomes their hearing, seeing, hand and foot. This is *al-takhalluq bi-akhlāqi l-lāh* (*Asfār*, iv. 2. 81–2).

This phrase, used by many philosophers and Sufis before Ṣadrā, refers to one's effort to imitate and eventually assume the Divine traits of intelligence, perfection and compassion. It can be translated literally as 'becoming ethical through the ethical qualities of God' but 'ethics' in its Arabic root is related to both nature and character. In a wider context, it refers to spiritual and moral qualities which an intelligent person is supposed to have. By striving to become 'Divine-like', the philosopher reaches for a fresh synthesis of the conceptual, moral and spiritual dimensions of reality.

This makes philosophy more than conceptual acuteness. It charges philosophical reflection with the task of seeing the reality of things as they are and acting accordingly. Philosophy as wisdom is expected to widen our horizon but its ultimate goal is to make us better human beings. But given the nature of the human state, becoming a better person means overcoming our own self and connecting with a higher principle that cannot be monopolized and manipulated by a self-deceiving ego. We can become truly 'human' only by trying to become 'Divine-like'. Assuming the traits of the Divine is to imitate the Divine to the extent to which it is possible for humans. This is the ultimate goal of philosophy and the proper definition of wisdom: 'The highest of the arts and the noblest of the deeds of the heart and the actions of one's capacity is the attainment of the art which some call wisdom and philosophy, and it is to be like God the Truth (*al-tashabbuh bi-l-ilāh al-ḥaqq*) and coming closer to Him to the extent possible for humans' (*Tafsīr*, vi. 3).

This moral-spiritual conclusion is in perfect harmony with the basic thrust of Ṣadrā's thought. For Ṣadrā, reality can best be understood by referring to the higher principles that sustain it. Existence, the cornerstone of Ṣadrean metaphysics, generates and sustains things but is never exhausted by them. When we deal with individual beings and entities, we are in fact encountering existence and its various modalities. Since the modalities in which existence manifests itself are as important as the principle of existence itself, we have to treat each being as a unique case of 'expanding existence' whose ultimate source is God Himself. Since beings have intrinsic intelligibility and order on the one hand, and let Being show itself through them on the other, Ṣadrā's view of the universe is necessarily anti-utilitarian. The utility of things is granted but this cannot define their true nature.

The same principle applies to knowledge: since knowledge comes about at the meeting point of subject and object and obtains completion through the unification of the knower and the known, instrumental rationality does not arise even as a possibility for Ṣadrā. Instrumental rationality reduces the primary function of reason to the efficient use of available means to reach our ends. But it says nothing about the content of our cognitive acts and their consequences. 'Rationality' as 'intelligibility' involves more than achieving our ends through systematic and logical procedures. The procedural definition of rationality gives us a skeleton to work with but cannot make a statement on either meaning or value. But if our survey of Ṣadrā's concept of reason and rationality is any indication, rationality as intelligibility is related to existence and its modalities in an essential way. That something is intelligible means that it has a certain order and structure by which we can understand it. Knowing is a way of discovering this order and structure. Ṣadra's philosophical reflections on existence and knowledge make it clear that we can seek to understand the world outside us but cannot claim to be the owners of it. This point of view allows neither an ontological hegemony nor epistemic imperialism for the knowing subject.

Knowledge as the highest virtue is eventually a means of attaining the Divine truth. For Ṣadrā, this is a thoroughly existential and spiritual experience – an experience that transforms our whole being and opens up infinitely new possibilities for us to reach our ultimate goal in this world. As Ṣadrā puts it, this is also the highest happiness and greatest liberation we can ever attain:

The most virtuous happiness, the most important means, and the chief of all beauties and virtues is attaining the wisdom of the Divine Truth and perfecting the power of thinking by acquiring the knowledge of real sciences and gnosis based on certainty. It is also perfecting the material intellects with the knowledge of God, His Qualities, His Rule and Dominion, the knowledge of the hereafter and its stations and degrees. It is through this knowledge that the human person becomes a traveller on the path of realized knowledge and turns in the direction of the Kaʿba of veritable knowledge and faith. He becomes liberated from the prison of events and disappointments and enters the paradise of happiness and comes to the proximity of the Infinitely Merciful. It is through this knowledge that we attain the knowledge of luminous words and spiritual essences and angelic lights, which are the cause of the knowledge of the Infinitely Merciful. As it is said in the ancient wisdom tradition: 'Whoever has known his own essence has become Divine-like', meaning that he has become a knower through the Lord, extinguished from himself and drowned in the witnessing of the beauty and majesty of the One. (*Maẓāhir*, 4)

6

Further reading and Works cited

Ṣadrā's life

Ibrahim Kalin, 'An Annotated Bibliography of the Works of Mullā Ṣadrā with a Brief Account of His Life' (2003) provides an annotated list of Ṣadrā's works with manuscript information and also a brief survey of Ṣadrā's life.

Nāhid Bāqirī Khurram-dashtī with Fāṭimah Aṣgharī, *Kitāb Shināsi-yi jāmiʿi Mullā Ṣadrā* (1378 SH/1999), contains information on manuscripts of Ṣadrā's works.

Sajjad H. Rizvi, *Mullā Ṣadrā Shīrāzī: His Life and Works and the Sources for Safavid Philosophy* (2007) is a detailed treatment of Ṣadrā's life and works with extensive annotations and manuscript details.

General works

Henry Corbin devoted a substantial section of his *En Islam Iranien* (1972) to a study of Ṣadrā's thought with a particular emphasis on his Shiʿi background. His 'La Place de Molla Sadra dans la philosophie iranienne' (1963) provides a general assessment of Ṣadrā's thought and its place in Persian Islamic philosophy.

Ibrahim Kalin, 'Mullā Ṣadrā' in *The Biographical Encyclopedia of Islamic Philosophy* (2006) is an overview of Ṣadrā's thought with references to earlier philosophers.

Muḥammad Kamal, *Mullā Ṣadrā's Transcendent Philosophy* (2006) is a philosophical study of the concepts of being, nature and knowledge in Ṣadrā. It also discusses the 'School of Isfahan' and Ṣadrā's departure from the Peripatetic and Illuminationist traditions.

Seyyed Hossein Nasr, *Ṣadr al-Dīn Shīrāzī and His Transcendent Theosophy* (1997) is an introduction to Ṣadrā's thought and the intellectual environment in which he flourished, and also gives a short list of Ṣadrā's works. His 'Mullā Ṣadrā: His Teachings' (1996) is an overview of Ṣadrā's thought and its place in Islamic philosophy.

Fazlur Rahman, *The Philosophy of Mullā Ṣadrā* (1976) is a detailed study of Ṣadrā's thought, focusing primarily on the discursive-analytical aspects of his works.

Jaʿfar Sajjādī, *Farhang-i istilāḥāt-i falsafī-yi Mullā Ṣadrā* ('Philosophical Glossary of Mullā Ṣadrā', 2000) is a dictionary of Ṣadrā's terminology with extensive quotes from his works.

Metaphysics and ontology

Alparslan Açıkgenç, *Being and Existence in Ṣadrā and Heidegger* (1993) is a comparative study of Ṣadrā's concept of *wujūd* and Martin Heidegger's *Dasein*, with particular focus on their ontology.

David Burrell, 'Existence Deriving from "the Existent": Mullā Ṣadrā's Dialectic with Ibn Sīnā and Ibn al-ʿArabī' (2005) is a translation of parts of Ṣadrā's *Asfār* and a commentary on Ṣadrā's terminology of existence.

Christian Jambet, *The Act of Being: The Philosophy of Revelation in Mullā Ṣadrā* (2006) is a condensed analysis of Ṣadrā's metaphysics within a religio-philosophical context.

Ibrahim Kalin, 'Between Physics and Metaphysics: Mullā Ṣadrā on Nature and Motion' (2003) analyses Ṣadrā's concept of 'substantial motion' within the context of his ontology and cosmology and describes the dynamic world-order Ṣadrā presents in his elaborate cosmology. His 'Mullā Ṣadrā on Theodicy and the Best of All Possible Worlds' (2007) examines Ṣadrā's defense of the Ghazālian position on the best of all of possible worlds. Kalin, 'From the Temporal Time to the Eternal Now: Ibn al-ʿArabī and Mullā Ṣadrā on Time' (2007) compares the concepts of time in Ibn ʿArabī and Mullā Ṣadrā and discusses the 'relativity' of time in their works.

Sajjad Rizvi, 'Mysticism and Philosophy: Ibn ʿArabī and Mullā Ṣadrā' (2005) provides an overview of the philosophical doctrines of the two philosophers. His *Mullā Ṣadrā and Metaphysics: Modulation of Being* (2009) is a thorough study of Ṣadrā's concept of existence and its modulation or gradation according to different degrees and modalities

Epistemology

Ibrahim Kalin, 'Mullā Ṣadrā's Realist Ontology and the Concept of Knowledge' (2004) analyses Ṣadrā's ontology and his attempt to reduce knowledge and cognition to existence and its modalities. His *Knowledge in Later Islamic Philosophy: Mullā Ṣadrā On Existence, Intellect and Intuition* (2010) is a detailed analysis of Ṣadrā's theory of knowledge in general and the unification of the intellect and the intelligible in particular. The book also discusses the implications of Ṣadrā's concept of knowledge for a number of problems in traditional metaphysics, ontology and spiritual quest.

Oliver Leaman, 'Mullā Ṣadrā, Perception and Knowledge by Presence' (2000) focuses on Ṣadrā's reworking of the Suhrawardīan notion of 'knowledge by presence' (*al-ʿilm al-ḥuḍūrī*). Mehdi Ha'iri Yazdi, *The Principles of Epistemology in Islamic Philosophy: Knowledge by Presence* (1992) is a detailed study and defence of 'knowledge by presence' as developed by Suhrawardī and Ṣadrā.

Morris Zailan, *Revelation, Intellectual Intuition and Reason in the Philosophy of Mullā Ṣadrā: An Analysis of the al-Ḥikmah al-ʿArshiyyah* (2003) studies, in this major work of Ṣadrā, certain aspects of his epistemology.

Other aspects of Ṣadrā's thought

Latimah-Parvin Peerwani, *On the Hermeneutics of the Light Verse of the Quran*, (2004) examines Ṣadrā's hermeneutical approach to understanding the Qurʾān and his use of the philosophical exegetical tradition. His 'Mind–Body Relationship according to Mullā Ṣadrā' (2005) looks at Ṣadrā's concept of existence to address the mind–body problem and attempts to give a 'holistic' account of the human soul.

James W. Morris, 'Mullā Ṣadrā's Conception of the *Barzakh* and the Emerging Science of Spirituality: The Process of Realization (*tahqīq*)' (2005) deals with an important aspect of Ṣadrā's spiritual cosmology and its relationship to human perfection.

WORKS CITED

Açıkgenç, Alparslan, *Being and Existence in Ṣadrā and Heidegger* (Kuala Lumpur: International Institute of Islamic Thought and Civilization, 1993).

Babayan, Kathryn, *Mystics, Monarchs and Messiahs: Cultural Landscapes of Early Modern Iran* (Cambridge, MA: Harvard University Press, 2002).

Browne, Edward G., *A Literary History of Persia* (Cambridge: Cambridge University Press, 1953).

Burrell, David, 'Existence Deriving from "the Existent": Mullā Ṣadrā's Dialectic with Ibn Sīnā and Ibn al-ʿArabī' in *Mulla Sadra's School and Western Philosophies*, 1 (Tehran, 2005).

Corbin, Henry, *En islam iranien: aspects spirituels et philosophiques* (Paris : Gallimard, 4 vols., 1974): iv. 54–122.

——, 'La Place de Molla Sadra dans la philosophie iranienne' *Studia Islamica*, 18 (1963): 81–113.

Dabashi, Hamid, 'Mīr Dāmād and the Founding of the "School of Isfahan" ' in Seyyed Hossein Nasr and Oliver Leaman (eds.), *A History of Islamic Philosophy* (London: Routledge, 1996), i. 597–634.

al-Fārābī, Abū Naṣr, *Kitāb al-Milla wa-nuṣūṣ ukhrā* (ed. Muḥsin Mahdi; Beirut: Dār al-Mashriq, 2nd edn., 1991).

Gleave, Robert, *Scripturalist Islam: The History and Doctrines of the Akhbārī Shīʿī School* (Leiden: Brill, 2007).

Hadot, Pierre, *Philosophy as a Way of Life: Spiritual Exercises from Socrates to Foucault* (transl. M. Chase; Oxford: Blackwell, 1995).

Halm, Heinz, *Shiʿism* (Edinburgh: Edinburgh University Press, 1991).

Ibn ʿArabī, *al-Futūḥāt al-Makkiyya* (Beirut: Dār al-Iḥyāʾ al-Turāth al-ʿArabī, 1997)

Ibn Sīnā, *Shifāʾ*, *Ṭabiʿiyyāt* (eds. I. Madkour and M. Qāsim; Cairo: Dār al-Kutub al-ʿArabī, 1960).

—, 'On the Rational Soul' in Dmitri Gutas, *Avicenna and the Aristotelian Tradition: Introduction to Reading Avicenna's Philosophical Works* (Leiden: Brill, 1988), 77–8.

Jambet, Christian, *The Act of Being: The Philosophy of Revelation in Mullā Ṣadrā* (transl. Jeff Fort; New York: Zone Books, 2006).

Kalin, Ibrahim, 'An Annotated Bibliography of the Works of Mullā Ṣadrā with a Brief Account of His Life', *Islamic Studies*, 421/1 (Spring 2003): 21–62.

—, 'From the Temporal Time to the Eternal Now: Ibn al-ʿArabī and Mullā Ṣadrā on Time', *Journal of the Muhyiddin ibn 'Arabi Society*, 41 (2007): 31–62 .

—, 'Between Physics and Metaphysics: Mullā Ṣadrā on Nature and Motion', *Islam and Science*, 1 (2003): 65–93.

—, 'Mullā Ṣadrā on Theodicy and the Best of All Possible Worlds', *Journal of Islamic Studies*, 18/2 (2007): 183–201.

—, *Knowledge in Later Islamic Philosophy: Mullā Ṣadrā on Existence, Intellect and Intuition* (New York: Oxford Univ. Press, 2010).

—, 'Mullā Ṣadrā', Oxford Bibliographies Online at http://oxfordbibliographiesonline.com/view/document/obo-9780195390155/obo-9780195390155-0053.xml

Kamal, Muḥammad, *Mullā Ṣadrā's Transcendent Philosophy* (Vermont: Ashgate, 2006).

Khamanei, *Ṣadrā* (Tehran: SIPRIn, 1379 SH).

Khurram-dashtī, Nāhid Bāqirī with Fāṭimah Aṣgharī, *Kitāb Shināsi-yi jāmīʿi Mullā Ṣadrā*, (Tehran: Bunyād-i Ḥikmat-i Islāmi-yi Ṣadrā (SIPRIn), 1378 SH/1999).

Leaman, Oliver, 'Mullā Ṣadrā, Perception and Knowledge by Presence', *Transcendent Philosophy*, 1/1 (2000).

Morris, James W., 'Mullā Ṣadrā's Conception of the *Barzakh* and the Emerging Science of Spirituality: The Process of Realization (*taḥqīq*)', *Mulla Sadra's School and Western Philosophies*, 10 (Tehran, 2005): 93–103.

Mujtabai, Fathullaj, *Hindu–Muslim Cultural Relations* (New Delhi: n.p., 1978; republished by the Iranian Institute of Philosophy, Tehran, 2007)

Naeem, Fuad, 'A Traditional Islamic Response to the Rise of Modernism' in Joseph Lumbard (ed.), *Islam, Fundamentalism, and the Betrayal of Tradition* (Bloomington, IN: World Wisdom, 2004), 79–116.

Nasr, Seyyed Hossein, 'Mullā Ṣadrā: His Teachings' in Nasr and Oliver Leaman (eds.), *History of Islamic Philosophy*, (London/New York: Routledge, 1996), 643–62.

——, *Ṣadr al-Dīn Shīrāzī and His Transcendent Theosophy* (Tehran: Institute for Humanities & Cultural Studies, 2nd edn., 1997).

——, *Three Muslim Sages* (New York: Caravan Books, 1997), 63–4.

——, 'The School of Isfahan' in M. M. Sharif (ed.), *A History of Muslim Philosphy* (Wiesbaden: Harrasowitz, 1966), ii. 904–32; reprinted in his *The Islamic Intellectual Tradition in Persia* (ed. Mehdi Amin Razavi; Curzon Press, 1996), 239–70.

——, 'The School of Isfahan Revisited' in his *Islamic Philosophy from its Origin to the Present: Philosophy in the Land of Prophecy* (Albany, NY: State University of New York Press, 2006), 209–21.

——, 'Spiritual Movements, Philosophy and Theology in the Safavid Period' in Peter Jackson and Laurence

Lockhart (eds.), *The Cambridge History of Iran* (Cambridge: Cambridge University Press, 1986), vi. 656–97.

Newman, A. J., 'Towards a Reconsideration of the Isfahan School of Philosophy: Shaykh Bahāʾī and the Role of the Ṣafavid ʿUlamāʾ', *Studia Iranica*, 15/2 (Paris, 1986): 165–99.

Otto, Rudolf, *Mysticism East and West* (New York: The Macmillan Co. Inc., 1960).

Peerwani, Latimah-Parvin, *On the Hermeneutics of the Light Verse of the Quran* (London: Saqi Books, 2004).

——, 'Mind–Body Relationship according to Mullā Ṣadrā', *Mulla Sadra's School and Western Philosophies*, 1 (2005, Tehran): 37–47.

Rahman, Fazlur, *The Philosophy of Mullā Ṣadrā* (Albany, NY: State University of New York Press, 1975).

Rizvi, Sajjad, 'Mysticism and Philosophy: Ibn ʿArabī and Mullā Ṣadrā' in Peter Adamson and Richard Taylor (eds.), *The Cambridge Companion to Arabic Philosophy* (Cambridge: The Cambridge University Press, 2005): 224–46.

——, *Mullā Ṣadrā Shīrāzī : His Life and Works and the Sources for Safavid Philosophy* (Oxford: *Journal of Semitic Studies, Supplement 18*, 2007).

——, *Mullā Ṣadrā and Metaphysics: Modulation of Being* (London: Routledge, 2009).

Sajjādī, Jaʿfar, *Farhang-i Istilāhāt-i Falsafi-yi Mullā Ṣadrā* ('Philosophical Glossary of Mullā Ṣadrā'), (Tehran, repr., 2000).

Suhrawardī, *Kitāb Ḥikmat al-ishrāq* in Henry Corbin (ed.), *Oeuvres Philosophiques et Mystiques* (Tehran: Imperial Iranian Academy of Philosophy, 1977). English transl. by John Walbridge and Hossein Ziai: *The Philosophy of Illumination* (Utah: Brigham Young University Press, 1999).

Whitehead, Alfred North, *Process and Reality. An Essay in Cosmology.* (Gifford Lectures, University of Edinburgh 1927–1928; Cambridge: Cambridge University Press, 1929).

Wittgenstein, Ludwig, *Philosophical Investigations* (transl. G. E. M. Anscombe; New York: Macmillan Publishing Co. Inc., 1968).

Yazdi, Mehdi Ha'iri, *The Principles of Epistemology in Islamic Philosophy: Knowledge by Presence* (Albany, NY: State University of New York Press, 1992).

Zailan, Morris, *Revelation, Intellectual Intuition and Reason in the Philosophy of Mullā Ṣadrā: An Analysis of the al-Ḥikmah al-Arshiyyah* (London: RoutledgeCurzon, 2003).

Index

al-Qummī, Qāḍī Saʿīd, 19
Qumshāʾī, Āqā Muḥammad Riḍā, 19
Qūnawī, Ṣadr al-Dīn, 21, 36, 38
Qurʾān: *passim*; as source of knowledge, 7, 25, 32, 46, 48, 55, 62, 64–5, 113, 132, 140, 158, 170
rabbāniyyūn ('those who follow the ways of the Lord'), 69, 71. *See also:* sages
Rāzī, Abū Bakr al-, 51
Rāzī, Fakhr al-Dīn, 121
reason, intellect (*al-ʿaql*): *passim*; discursive, 7–8, 30, 45–7, 49, 56, 69; human (unaided), 8, 14, 46–7, 54–5, 58–61, 75, 103, 123, 163, 165, 170, 175; and revelation, 6, 22, 55, 66, 69, 135–8, 153. *See also:* knowledge
'relation' (*iḍāfa*), 121
'representation' (*irtisām*), 58, 83, 97, 129–30, 133–5
resurrection, 27, 29–32, 48, 80, 159–62. *See also:* afterlife
revelation (*waḥy*), 4, 6, 22, 31, 50, 55–9, 65, 69, 107, 119, 135–8, 169–70, 172, 175
Sabziwārī, Mullā Hādī, 19
Ṣadrā's *Four Journeys* (*Asfār arbaʿa*), 8, 10, 15–17, 21, 23, 25, 28–31, 47–8, 50, 53, 62, 64, 66, 76, 81, 84–6, 90–1, 94–6, 101–4, 108, 112–15, 122, 125, 129–32, 134–5, 139–40, 142–4, 146–7, 150, 153–4, 156–9, 164, 168
sages: 26, 43, 52, 132, 173; of the Lord, 71; *ʿurafāʾ*, 90
scholars of the skin or surface (*ʿulamā-yi qishr*), 15
'secondary intelligible' (*maʿqūl thānī*), 57, 82, 91
self-effusion (*fayḍ*), 108–9
self-evident (*badihi*), 82, 120
self-knowledge, 133–5, 148
sense organs, 45, 75, 79, 86, 110, 122–3, 127
Shāh ʿAbbās I, 13, 35
Shāh Ismāʿīl, 34–5
Shāh Ṣafī, 15, 35
Shiʿitization (*tashayyuʿ*), 34–5
Simnānī, ʿAlāʾ al-Dawla, 89
soul as 'corporeal in origination', 'spiritual in subsistence', 5, 145–8, 160–2
spiritual practice (*riyāḍa*), 32, 38, 55–67
substance: 1, 7, 20, 29, 42, 50, 72–3, 80–2, 85–7, 91–2, 95, 100, 108, 110–17, 119, 121, 124–6, 136; *jawhar*, 143–7, 151, 161–2
substantial motion (*al-ḥarakat al-jawhariyya*), 5–7, 20, 29, 109–16, 147, 157, 162, 169
'Sufi imaginings', 67
Sufism and Shiʿism, 36–9
Suhrawardī, 18, 21, 24, 38, 41, 56–8, 85, 91, 114–15, 124, 132–4, 170, 174. *See also:* Illumination
Ṭābaṭabāʾī Muḥammad Ḥusayn, 19
tasting (*dhawq*), 48–9, 61–4, 96, 126, 135, 137
'temporal origination of the world' (*al-ḥuduth al-dahrī*), 29, 31, 41–3, 106–8, 112–13, 117, 172
Thānwī, Ashraf ʿAlī, 22

'theoretical consideration' (*iʿtibār*), 71, 73, 78, 86, 89–90, 98–9, 112, 130, 134, 143, 158
'theoretical Sufism' (*ʿirfān-i naẓarī*), 37–8
theosophers (*mutaʾallihīn*), 18, 359, 90
time (*zamān*), 6, 30, 42, 70, 107–8, 110–11, 117, 139, 154, 165, 172
transcendence (*tanzīh*), 27, 78, 88
Transcendent Wisdom (*al-ḥikmat al-mutaʿāliya*), 9, 3, 8, 10, 21, 28, 31, 38, 43–6, 50, 54, 64–5, 98, 101
transmigration' (*tanāsukh*), 30
transmitted sciences (*al-ʿulum al-naqliyya*), 14, 26–7, 44
traveller (*sālik*), 29, 39, 43, 166
'true demonstration' (*al-burhān al-ḥaqīqī*), 8, 47
unaided reason, 58–61
'unification of the intellect and the intelligible' (*ittihād al-ʿāqil wa-l-maʿqūl*), 123–4, 169
'unity-in-plurality' (*al-waḥda fī l-kathrā*), 72, 86, 100
univocal predication (*ḥaml bi-l-tawatiʿ*), 72, 86, 100
value, 73–4, 79, 148, 165
via negativa, 75
Whitehead, A. N., 6, 174
'witnessing' (*mushāhada*), 53, 59, 61–3, 86, 125, 130, 140–1, 166; 'direct w.' (*shuhūd ʿaynī*) 53, 61, 63, 86, 130, 134, 140 ;'witnessing based on unveiling' (*al-shuhūd al-kashfī*), 47. *See also*: 'illuminative presence'
Wittgenstein: 93,. 99, 133–4, 176; his ladder, 51, 163
Yoga-Vasishtha, 43
Zunūzī, Mullā ʿAbdullāh, 19